A VANISHED HAND
My Autograph Album

A Vanished Hand
My Autograph Album
Memories of the 1950s

ANTHONY RUDOLF

Shearsman Books

Published in the United Kingdom in 2013 by
Shearsman Books
50 Westons Hill Drive
Emersons Green
BRISTOL BS16 7DF

Shearsman Books Ltd Registered Office
30–31 St. James Place, Mangotsfield, Bristol BS16 9JB
(this address not for correspondence)

www.shearsman.com

ISBN 978-1-84861-292-1

Typeset in the United Kingdom by Antony Gray

For
Nathaniel and Helen
and
my granddaughter Leah
and
Naomi and Jason
and
my grandson Charlie

Acknowledgments:
Mark Pirie for publishing an extract
in *Broadsheet* (New Zealand)

Naomi Rudolf and Ruth Blane for
Alma Cogan tombstone photographs

I would like to thank four people,
Gabriel Levin, Miriam Neiger,
Rabbi Frank Hellner and, in particular,
Rabbi Howard Cooper, for their thoughts
about the Hebrew wording on
Alma Cogan's tombstone

Contents

. . . O for the touch of a vanished hand,
And the sound of a voice that is still!

TENNYSON, 'Break, Break, Break'

Introduction

There is a powerful moment in *The Glass Menagerie*, when Jim, the gentleman caller, brought home by his friend Tom under false pretences, signs with a great flourish the high-school yearbook of Tom's sister Laura who, it turns out, had loved him when he was the star student. The irony is that Jim too is a loser who, unlike his fellow warehouse worker Tom (a secret poet and alter ego of the playwright, which implies redemption despite the utter bleakness of the play), will never escape his destiny; for a brief moment, however, he rides high, monarch of all he surveys, that is to say, of poor crippled Laura tied to her impossible mother in a *ménage à deux*. I saw the Young Vic production of the play with Paula [Rego], a fellow fan of Tennessee Williams, a few days before adding these words to my essay. A high-school yearbook is not an autograph album, but it is a 'keepsake' volume of an important kind, more usual in North America, though now becoming more common here. The first time I saw the play was in the 1980s at the beautiful Edwardian theatre in Portsmouth when I was the guest of a friend who was starring in it, Susannah York. Susannah, who sadly died on the day that I am writing this very paragraph and with whom I had hoped to discuss the Young Vic production, got me signatures for my son's autograph album when he was young, including Peter O'Toole, a notoriously difficult catch. She also signed copies of her books (*In Search of Unicorns* and *Lark's Castle*) for my two children, but that's different from albums. Nicholas Humphrey and I visited her on different days in hospital during her final illness. She told Nick that she had had a good innings. Despite the use of this metaphor, she was not a cricket fan. Nobody's perfect.

In his book *Consciousness Regained*, Nick Humphrey has a chapter on collecting, how the classic versions of the hobby (or obsession) depend on completing sets, on variations and so on, what Gerard Manley Hopkins called 'rhyme', or 'likeness tempered with difference'. This could apply to autographs, but not in my case, since I was eclectic and not specifically collecting film stars or Middlesex cricketers. Walter Benjamin's words are germane to this exploration of my quondam self: 'Every passion borders on the chaotic, but the collector's passion borders on the chaos of memories'. Benjamin was referring to adult collectors, specifically to collectors of books. But the 'chaos of memories' is what floods back to me as I explore my long lost and newly found autograph album. My autograph collecting, however, cannot be dignified with the word passion because I managed to obtain only sixty signatures during a period of less than ten years. There was competition from my stamp collecting and my cigarette card collecting, the latter entirely dependent upon the largesse of smokers and the junk-shop in Temple Fortune, the former upon letters received by parents and grandparents and from specialist outlets like Stanley Gibbons in the Strand. Unlike my stamp album, with its rows of stamps as obedient as toy soldiers, the autographs are indeed chaotically ranged and (dis) ordered. I fear that the meanings discerned from the gestalt will be as disordered as those called for by Rimbaud in his famous letter of May 13, 1871 (the first of the two remarkable 'lettres du voyant'), sixty quantums interacting in a miniature cosmos, which as a participant observer I still harbour hopes of bringing to order, although I am only too aware of the risks. Note the conclusion of 'The Idea of Order at Key West', where Wallace Stevens addresses and implicitly criticises the literary critic and ideological lover of order, Ramon Fernandez:

> Oh! Blessed rage for order, pale Ramon,
> The maker's rage to order words of the sea,
> Words of the fragrant portals, dimly-starred,
> And of ourselves and of our origins,
> In ghostlier demarcations, keener sounds.

After all, as Stevens put it in 'Mr Burnshaw and the Statue' (in *Opus Posthumous*), a lesser poem than 'The Idea of Order at Key West',

> . . . even disorder may,
> So seen, have an order of its own . . .

Or, if you like,

> . . . things as they are
> Are changed upon the blue guitar

to quote Stevens again, this time from one of his two most famous poems. By a strange coincidence, I can claim a connection to Ramon – I knew his son, Dominique – and to Stanley Burnshaw: I corresponded with him over the use of one of his poems in an anthology. The nearest I got to Stevens himself, one of my favourite poets of all time, was to be driven past his house in Hartford, Connecticut, by another translator of Yves Bonnefoy, Richard Stamelman.

Will my grandchildren Charlie and Leah collect autographs when they are teenagers? Or is this a practice from the childhood world of one who, for example, attended that classic annual event of the 1950s, the Schoolboys Exhibition at the Royal Horticultural Hall in Westminster, a jamboree no longer possible to imagine? On my desk is the album itself, a veritable talisman, unadulterated testimony from a world that is lost and gone forever, and most of the autographers dead. '…. O for the touch of a vanished hand, / And the sound of a voice that is still!', wrote Tennyson. Strictly speaking, it should be 'signature album', since an autograph is any piece of hand-writing. However, let's stick with the version familiar from childhood when youngsters bought or were given a notebook with 'autographs' or 'autograph album' on the cover. Mine, after a vanishing act of thirty years (the length of time I have lived in my post-marital flat), is a treasure trove of nostalgia which I thought I would never see again. The other day I was in the shared attic above my flat and knocked over a box of old papers. I brought the whole box downstairs, enjoyed going through the papers, put a few aside grateful that I had kept them, and threw away most of the rest. There, at the bottom of the box, was the album. It is not, however, a purpose-printed album but an ordinary hard-cover notebook, the cover bluey-green. I would never have thought of adopting and adapting an ordinary notebook for my autographs. After all, I had a proper stamp album. The notebook would have been my father's idea. I am racking my brains as to why we did not buy me a proper album. I doubt that the reason was to save money although my father, generous with pounds, could be mean with pennies and, in any case, this notebook probably cost around the same amount as an album. Many of the signatures were written on pieces of paper which I then glued into the notebook. But surely I could have stuck them into a proper album. Unless the albums on sale in Market Place NW11, probably in Ellingtons the newsagent and stationer, were too small. Too small for what? Well, the first item in the album (on what would have been about the twentieth page, the earlier pages having been scissored out) takes up the whole page because it is a signed photograph. Is that a clue? Did I possess this and other full-page items before I owned the notebook and discovered that they would not fit into a regular album? Why have those pages been cut out? Did the notebook already belong to me or one of my parents and was no longer needed for its original purpose? That would make sense. In those days, people were thriftier with possessions; waste was not encouraged. We will come on to the first signature in a moment. Let's begin at the beginning, which is the inside front cover, since there is nothing on the front.

Inside Front Cover

Two pieces of paper are glued onto the inside front cover of my album. The first covers the entire board and says 'AUTO-GRAPH ALBUM' twice, top left and bottom right. Glued on top of it, along the diagonal, is a rectangular piece of paper on which is written: THIS ALBUM BELONGS TO A. RUDOLF / IF FOUND PLEASE RETURN TO: 41, MIDDLEWAY, HAMPSTEAD / GARDEN SUBURB, N.W.11 / PHONE: SPEedwell 7937 (my mother's phone number in various incarnations for nearly seventy years). The handwriting on this is more mature than the 2 x 2 words on the lower sheet, which may enable me to date the beginning and end of my collecting phase. I have been able to unpeel much of the lower sheet from the inside cover, allowing me to read what is written there. Its inflexible arrangement — since it is a contents list and not the index it claims to be itself— explains why the early pages of the album were torn out:

INDEX

Actors	1	Cyclists	9
Artists	2	Footballers	10
Athletes	3	Golfers	11
Boxers	4	Hockey	12
Comedians	5	Jockeys	13
Composers	6	Motor Cyclists	14
Cricketers	7 & 8	Politicians	15

Radio & TV Stars	16	[second row]
Rowers	17	Table Tennis Players 22
Royalty	18	Tennis Players 23
Rugger	19	Writers 24
Singers	20	Extra 25 & 26
Swimmers	21	

It would appear that the number of autographs overran the pages allotted, so I tore out the pages and started again. Four of the autographs have been scissored out of those early pages and glued onto cards and the card glued onto the new page. What happened to the others? Some may have become unglued from the cards they were on and were re-glued by me onto new pages, others perhaps swapped. There are several categories listed but I have no autographs pertaining to them: what in the name of memory became of the artists, composers, golfers, hockey players, jockeys, motor cyclists, rowers, royalty, rugger players? This is a major league mystery. They can't all have been swopped. There is only one illegible signature in the book, and it definitely belongs to a cricketer. It is inconceivable that this is a wish list – it is too specific. Also I had no interest in rugger or rowers or hockey, to name only three, so somehow, somewhere I must have obtained autographs of famous players.

Inside Back Cover

Glued along the edge to the inside back cover is a piece of paper, the writing upside down when the book is the right way up; on it is written in pencil 'For SWOPPING' and inked in a box: 'DUPLICATES AND UNWANTED AUTOGRAPHS'. Only one name is written there, Alma Cogan's, which suggests that I had two copies since I still have one in the book. Inside the folder created by the piece of paper are two signatures carefully cut out from a scorecard or other cricket document, headed Worcestershire, and their names written by me alongside the faded pencilled handwriting: J. Flavell and L. Devereux. Such was the hold on my memory of my seemingly lost autograph album that on one of the occasions I met Harold Pinter — it was a July 14 gathering (2004 or 2005) at the French ambassador's house — when, inevitably, the conversation turned to cricket, I told Pinter about my swops, mentioning Jack Flavell of Warwickshire, and would he consider a swop. Quick as a Denis Compton leg sweep, he said 'Worcestershire'. I should point out that Devereux and Flavell were not *heroes* of mine and, clearly I obtained their autographs — undoubtedly at Lords and probably sometime between 1957 and 1959 — in order to swop them. Not really an insult, is it? More like a compliment. I would have swopped both of them for Bill Edrich, who was a minor hero — because he played for Middlesex and by association with Denis Compton — even though I was cross with him for refusing to give me his autograph. Edrich was well known for this.

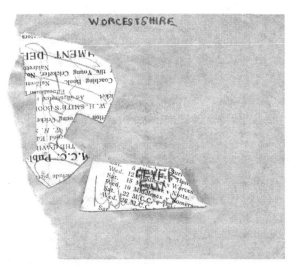

J. Flavell and L. Devereux

My other Pinter story happened at a charity dinner where, as the guest of Musa Farhi, I found myself at a good table sitting next to the playwright. 'When are you next going to write a full-length play?' I asked politely and out of genuine curiosity. 'All my plays are full length', he replied with mock gravity, before explaining that he had no plans to write a long play. As for Pinter's autograph, and those of other famous people, I have plenty of those in letters received over the years in my capacity as editor and translator. But obviously I no longer 'collect autographs'. At a certain age, nothing beats the thrill of meeting someone whose autograph you genuinely want. So, during which years was I collecting the signatures? We shall see. I have already alluded to the competing collections: my stamp collection began and ended earlier than the autograph album. I was not to know that I myself would one day end up on a postage stamp, as Mr Rochester in Paula Rego's Jane Eyre series. As for the cigarette cards, I have more to say about those in my book *The Arithmetic of Memory*.

Written on the inside back cover itself are two lists, the first one headed family. In the first column against 'ME' is my own signature followed by the signatures of my father and mother against 'DADDY' and 'MUMMY'. In the second column labelled '2nd' and '3rd' are two more of my own signatures, each more mature in writing and therefore later than the earlier one. The lettering of the first signature is compatible with a finding concerning Margaret Lockwood which we will come to. The final signature, 'Ruth Rudolf' is next to where I have written 'Ruth'. Ruth, the oldest of my three sisters and born in 1945 when I had just turned three, was probably nine or ten when she wrote it. Mary and Annie, born in 1951 and 1953, have not signed the book, either because they were still too young by the time I stopped collecting autographs, or because there was no more room, since I drew a line and wrote out another contents list or index. Looking again at the inside front cover, I would guess that the list was written when I was thirteen or fourteen, the rectangular strip when I was sixteen or seventeen, and the three signatures on the inside back cover when I was eight and ten and twelve. This dating, however, is open to reassessment since I now notice that the third one is an imitation of my father's signature. A preliminary thought prior to examining all the evidence would be that I began collecting in 1950 or 1951 when I was eight and ended in 1959, at latest December 1960 when I left school for what was not yet known as a gap year – in Paris – and then my three years in Cambridge.

The second list of names is headed 'List of Autographs (or Autographed Photographs)' and sub-headed to the left: 'A =Stage' / 'S=Sport' / 'P=Politician'. There are twenty-six names, at which point there is no more space. Typically, I had not taken this into consideration when embarking on this list. To this day, I have difficulty in negotiating space (except when parking a car, one of my few practical skills and a valuable one in downtown

The inside back cover

London) and time (except oddly enough when guessing the exact time, something which has never come in useful). I always underestimate or overestimate the time needed to accomplish a task. Still and all, I wonder how many of the names in the second list, and indeed the other names in the album itself, mean anything to younger readers. The list is not alphabetical, the three categories are mixed up: it is not chronological, as the rest of this book will reveal, although traces of the order remain. It has no discernible logic. There is reason to believe that Margaret Lockwood's was my first autograph and her name at the head of the list probably reflects that. Note that 'S' for Stage has been crossed out against her name and 'A' for Actors has been substituted, presumably to avoid confusion with Sport. There is one politician (P). Apart from the last six names, everyone is categorised. I see that I started out writing both names and then resorted to initials until Herbert Lom, who was allowed his first name; I then reverted to initials for Cogan and Vaughan before listing three cricketers merely by their surname. Warr was a 'gentleman', as in the 'Gentlemen versus Players' fixture; there was also a team called Gentlemen of Ireland. Parks and Thomson (misspelt as Thompson) were 'players', so, according to the convention of the day, J. J. Warr, still alive at the time of writing. Parks J. M. (ditto) and Thomson I. (deceased), deserve an apology.

		[second row]	
A	Margaret Lockwood	J. Wade	S
S	Jean Desforges	D. Bennett	S
S	Vic Herman	D. Bowen	S
S	Jack Hobbs	G. Iden	S
S	Reg Harris	E. Allan	
S	Alex Forbes	B. Wright	S
P	E. Shinwell	L. Compton	S
S	J. Logie	Herbert Lom	
A	M. Bygraves	A. Cogan	
A	S. Eaton	F. Vaughan	
S	J. Leach	Parks	
S	T. Lawton	Thompson	
		Warr	

The Autographs (1)

There are sixty autographs, some of which were obtained for me by well connected third parties, some I got by writing directly to the famous person, some as a result of personal encounter. The first page is entirely taken up with a signed photograph of the former world light heavyweight champion boxer (1948–1950), Freddie Mills, on which I have written 'now on 6.5 Special', and which is glued onto the page, like many of my autographs. I have written about my attendance at, indeed appearance on, this early BBC pop music programme, probably in 1958, in *The Arithmetic of Memory*. There are clips of the programme on YouTube but not, sadly, the one I was on. I once saw Mills at the top end of Charing Cross road, outside the nightclub he owned. A swift search in Google reveals that he may have committed suicide for fear of being killed by the Kray brothers, which I will leave readers to follow up if they want to. On the whole, I will rely on my memory and use the Internet to check queries where necessary and to report the occasional fascinating detail. Readers may want to investigate anything of specialised interest, although we should all beware of urban myths in this territory. I cannot remember if I asked Mills for his autograph and was directed to the club desk for a photo, or if I wrote to him care of somewhere or other. Not being a table tennis, soccer, cricket or tennis player, he was, by definition, not a major hero, although I had boxed at two of my schools and sometimes listened to live broadcasts of fights, setting my alarm for three in the morning when the fight was in New York.

The second autograph is slipped in after the Freddie Mills page, but not stuck down. This is significant because of the date. The piece of paper which is about three inches square is headed 'MEMO FROM EDDIE CANTOR' and the message reads: 'All good wishes Eddie Cantor March 10, 1959'. The fact that the autograph is not stuck into the notebook suggests to me that I was already losing interest in the collection and could not be bothered to secure the name through the permanence of glue. Perhaps it is the final autograph I collected. I never met Cantor and no longer recall who obtained it for me. A famous vaudeville performer and film star, he (and George Jessel) had turned down the role in *The Jazz Singer* which Al Jolson made famous. Is it a coincidence that all three candidates for the blackface role were Jewish? The main candidate for signature obtainer is my parents' friend Joe Pole, who had been Charlie Chaplin's secretary and later worked in public relations for United Artists. A Glaswegian Jewish autodidact, his two sons were brilliant academics, Jack and David Pole, historian and philosopher respectively. It was at Joe and Phoebe Pole's that I first met Sir Nicholas Serota, then Nicholas Serota. Although neither of us recalls this meeting, my mother did. When I introduced her to him at the Marlborough Gallery at a private view of a Paula Rego exhibition, she said: 'I remember you Nicky Serota, in short trousers, at the Poles' house. Anthony was too old to play with you' (and indeed Nick was and remains four years younger than me.) A signed message from Eddie is worth something on Ebay to collectors of Hollywood memorabilia. No doubt my whole album is an asset but I would prefer not to need to sell it. One day, with luck, it will join my son's autograph album as a family heirloom.

FREDDIE MILLS

Freddie Mills who held the World, British, Empire and European light-heavy weight championships. He came to prominence when he beat Len Harvey in 1942 for the British and Empire championships, his first title fight. In 1948 he won the World Championship at White City from Gus Lesnevich which he held until Joey Maxim took it from him in January, 1950. The other titles he held until he retired.

MEMO FROM
EDDIE CANTOR

Eddie Cantor

Reg Harris and Vic Herman are on the next page. I remember deciding to have mini-heroes in sports other than table-tennis, tennis, soccer and cricket, which were the *topoi* or *loci* of my major heroes. For example, there were Split Waterman in speedway racing and Reg Harris in cycling. The signed photograph of Harris, which I would have written off for, reads: 'Naturally, I always ride a BROOKS Saddle – the finest in the world' (Mel Brooks' *Blazing Saddles* came much later), followed by 'says Reg. Harris', with a full stop after his first name, and then 'World's Professional Sprint Champion'. The photo is courtesy of the *Daily Graphic*. Harris was professional champion in 1950, 1951 and 1954. These were the years when Denis Compton, the David Beckham of his day, was advertising Brylcreem. Yet

"Naturally,
I always ride
a BROOKS
Saddle -
the finest
in the world"
says Reg. Harris

World's Professional
Sprint Champion

Photo by Courtesy of "Daily Graphic"

Reg Harris

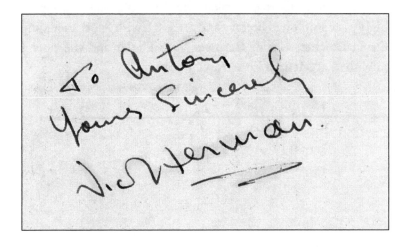

only a few sportsmen benefited from the additional income, unlike today. Kevin Pietersen is the current and fourth face of Brylcreem, following Compton, the Fulham footballer Johnny Haynes and David Beckham. Brooks Saddles, like Brylcreem, survives, but the *Daily Graphic* is long gone. Below Reg Harris is what looks like the back of a visiting card with the message: 'To Antony Yours Sincerely Vic Herman'. Spelling my first name without an 'h' annoys me as much as spelling my surname with a 'ph', but I would still have been pleased to have the autograph of a great boxer who fought for but lost the world fly-weight in 1952. 'Turning pro in 1947, he created a sensation by playing the bagpipes into the ring while wearing the Jewish Star of David on his trunks'. Herman was also a painter. The best painting on his website is of himself in later years, no longer lean and fit. A Gorbals orphan, he joins the select group of highly accomplished literary and artistic Jewish Scots, including David Daiches, Chaim Bermant, Ivor Cutler and the poet I published at Menard Press, A. C. Jacobs.

The Autographs (2)
Table Tennis

On the next page, a left-hand page, are two table-tennis players, against whose almost illegible signatures I have written their names: A. Ehrlich and Z. Berczik. These names are written straight onto the page, meaning I took my album with me to the championship venue, in this instance Manor Place Baths in Southwark. I also went to Wembley and other venues. As I have already touched on in *The Arithmetic of Memory*, to this day I dream table tennis, with its wondrous balletic rhythms and speed, and me playing with a grace I lack at the table or on the dance floor. It was the only sport I fantasised champion status for myself. At Cambridge I had won the freshman cup awarded by my college but, unlike my exact contemporary Howard Jacobson, I never played for the university. Writing is one thing (moi competitive?), but I shall never beat him at table-tennis, the bastard. Like the boxer Vic Herman's life, that of Alojzy (Alex) Ehrlich, a top Polish player, was amazing in ways that would one day interest me as a writer on, among other things, Jewish issues. As a teenager Ehrlich learned his skills in Hasmonea, a Jewish youth club in Lwow, the easternmost capital of the provinces making up the Austro-Hungarian empire, which is now the most important city in western Ukraine. The six foot four tall Ehrlich, who won the English open in 1935/6 and 1950/1, was said to speak

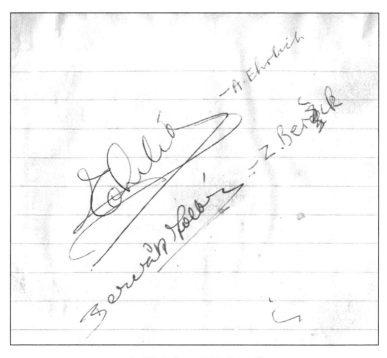

A. Ehrlich and Z. Berczik

fifteen languages badly (six more than my grandfather, also from that part of the world) and had such long arms he could scratch his knee without bending his back.

The facts in this section come mainly from a hilarious interview with Ehrlich in *Sports Illustrated* by a great USA table tennis player, Dick Miles (cross checked with other reports of the game. Once or twice I suspect, *se non e vero e molto ben trovato*). During the men's team event (The Swaythling Cup) in the Prague world championships of 1936, the first point of Ehrlich's game against the Romanian Paneth Farcas lasted two hours twelve minutes – the ball crossed the net more than twelve thousand times – as he sought to wear down his opponent from the word go. Ehrlich was playing with a huge 'chiseller's' bat (the bat can or could then be of any size). He switched to playing left-handed when his right arm got tired. Late in the point, his captain thoughtfully set up a chess game to keep him from getting bored. Ehrlich thought he had a winning position (involving a rook and a knight), but the game had to be abandoned when a hastily convened emergency meeting of the International Table Tennis Association returned to the arena so that the Polish delegate, one Alojzy Ehrlich, could be consulted about the game he was playing in. At this point (as it were), the point ended when Ehrlich for the first time sent the ball to Farcas's backhand, throwing him.

During the second and final point, which lasted twenty minutes, a member of the Polish team 'without realizing the psychological effect it would have on Paneth, reached down into an equipment bag and pulled out a knife, a long loaf of bread and a two-foot Polish sausage. He started slicing sandwiches, which he offered to Ehrlich. Another player filled cups from a huge coffee thermos. Paneth, who could see all this from his position at the table, must have assumed that the Poles were preparing for a winter siege' and began to mumble that Ehrlich was trying to drive him crazy. For the first and last time in his career he started attacking but finally snapped when he failed to get past Ehrlich's defences. He ran screaming from the court. There were two umpires, the first retired because his neck was locked to one side, the second was summoned home for dinner. Were there more than two umpires in the Timeless Test, which took place in Durban three years later, in March 1939?

You could describe Ehrlich and Farcas as defensive players (which is what I am), although they were undoubtedly not as entertaining to watch as my favourite player Richard Bergmann, whom I saw at Wembley towards the end of his career. The rules were changed, surprise surprise, after the Ehrlich-Farcas match. Although liberated from Dachau, Ehrlich had spent a long time in Auschwitz where apparently he was spared from the gas chambers at the last minute because a guard recognised him as a sports champion. Such prisoners were sometimes taken outside the camp to show locals that prisoners were in good shape. But the same report also says that this man who was well over six foot tall weighed only thirty seven kilos on liberation. It strikes me that the long point of 1936 would make a wonderful film (possibly animated) in the right directorial hands. Howard Jacobson and Jerome Charyn, a ranking veteran at the sport and novelist who wrote a fine book on the subject (*Sizzling Chops and Devilish Spins*) could star as Ehrlich and Farcas, who was Jewish and, amazingly, was, like Ehrlich, a survivor of the camps. Could their patience and defensive skills have helped?

Zoltán Berzcik was a classy Hungarian player much younger than the players I favoured such as Johnny Leach, Bergmann and Ehrlich. In the mid 1930s, my uncle Isadore played against Bohumil Vana in the East End at Brady's Jewish youth club, where the great Czechoslovak player, using an HP sauce bottle as a bat, took on all comers. On the right hand page of my album, facing the signatures of Ehrlich and Berzcik, is Johnny Leach himself, the only British-born men's singles world champion. Bergmann, a Jewish refugee to the UK from Vienna, was also world champion, twice before the war and, as a naturalised Briton, twice after the war. Leach, who won his second men's singles world championship in 1951, was one of the two last world champions before the penholder Asian revolution created a dominance that has lasted for decades, with only five or six winners from countries outside Asia, three of them Swedish. The first sponge rubber world champion was Hiroji Satoh of Japan in 1952. By 1959 everybody used sponge. I met Johnny Leach at one or two of the annual *Eagle* table-tennis competitions held in the hall at St Brides Church, off Fleet Street, probably in 1956 and/or 1957. I assume his presence was needed (whether paid or unpaid) as a famous player figurehead, to publicise the competition, in which I never got past the third round. *Eagle* was the favoured comic among the middle classes, the only approved one in our house. It was at this event that I got Leach's autograph, which was originally written in the album then cut out and pasted onto card and repasted onto this new page.

Johnny Leach

Even though Leach, with Richard Bergmann, was one of my heroes, I will not hold against him the last sentence of a Pathe newsreel made in 1960 at Butlins, where he was running a coaching scheme with another champion, Diane Rowe of the Rowe twins: 'Not all our much maligned youth are teddy boys and beatniks'. Too old to be an ageing hippy, and the same age as Bob Dylan and Paul McCartney, I sometimes categorise myself as a second generation beatnik and could spend several paragraphs analysing or deconstructing the mentality behind that particular idea, since a teddy boy I wasn't. Suffice it to say, within a few years the scriptwriter would have had to write 'mods and rockers' (as in the new film version of *Brighton Rock* set in 1964) and after that 'hippies and skinheads', and also within a few years such a differentiation between clean-living boy-scout table tennis players and the surrounding youth rabble would not have been made. That newsreel was made in the year that *Lady Chatterley's Lover* was found not guilty. In 1963, the Beatles' first two LPs came out, and it was not only Beethoven who rolled over. I found my feet (taught the twist by AFJ) and lost my virginity (with somebody else).

The Autographs (3)

Below the signature of Johnny Leach is that of 'Alex Forbes, Arsenal FC', stuck on in the same way as Leach's. Forbes was a tough, old-fashioned wing-half, a precursor of later midfield players like Nobby Stiles. Forbes, a Scottish international, played in Arsenal's FA cup-winning team of 1950. I watched that cup final at my grandparents' house in Stoke Newington, which taking place on a Saturday proves that my paternal grandparents were less strictly religious than the maternal side, who would

Jack Hobbs

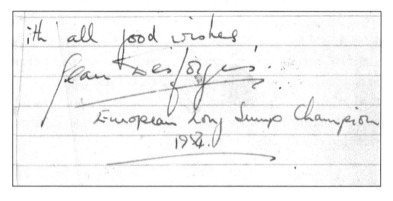

Jean Desforges

never have switched on a TV (not that they had one) on the Jewish Sabbath. Alex Forbes was the owner of a cafeteria on the corner of Blackfriars Bridge diagonally opposite Unilever House, which was next door my school, and the cafeteria was where I got his autograph. On the next right hand page is the signature of one of the greatest batsmen who ever lived, Jack Hobbs. Hobbs' sports shop in Fleet Street was only a little further away from the school than Forbes' café. I requested his autograph on the occasion I went in there to buy a pair of Eton Fives gloves, my winter sport of choice after abandoning rugby. Sports shop? Cafeteria? Skip the disquisition on the rewards of present-day players and hop or jump to the next signature.

Heaven knows where I met Jean Desforges, whose autograph on the same page helpfully reads: 'with all good wishes, Jean Desforges. European Long Jump Champion, 1954'. I never went to athletics meetings. Perhaps there was an athletes' stand at the Schoolboys Exhibition. Somewhere I have a sketch of me done at the Exhibition.

Following a blank left-hand page, we come to 'Best Wishes Shirley Eaton 1955' and 'To Anthony Best Wishes Margaret Lockwood', both on coloured paper pasted onto card pasted onto the page. As with Jean Desforges, I have no recollection where I met Shirley Eaton. Indeed she may have been obtained for me by a third party like my Uncle Leon or Joe Pole. A glance at her filmography suggests that 1955 was the year she became famous, starring for the first time, in *The Love Match*. Her

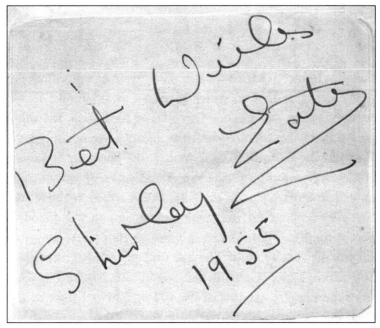

Shirley Eaton

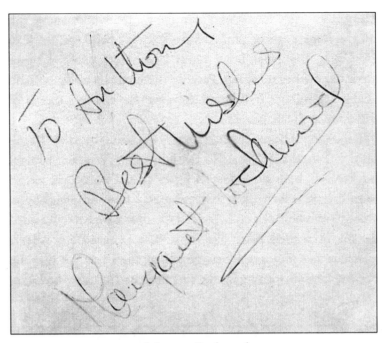

Margaret Lockwood

previous film appearance was as a sixth-former ('uncredited') in *The Belles of St Trinians*, which gives me an additional reason to want to see this Launder and Gilliat film again, the other reason being the school's similarity, in my imagination, to the English school Paula [Rego] went to in Portugal, St Julian's at Carcavelos. Sandra Caron too, Alma's sister, of whom more anon, had a small part in this film. Eaton retired at thirty two, best remembered for her goldfingered or rather goldbodied part in the Bond film: 'A career is a career, but you're a mother till you die', as she put it. She had studied at Aida Foster Stage School in Golders Green in the early 1950s. Maybe I saw her from the upstairs window of the 102 or 58 bus I took to and from the station everyday during the two-stage journey to my prep school in St Johns Wood and then City of London School

on Victoria Embankment. Yes yes, the trope of 'Maybe I saw
. . . ' is empty, since even if I did, it could not have registered.
This particular trope is the weakest form of vicarious glory
imaginable. The best that can be said for it is that I have used
my imagination to analyse its properties.

I have already touched on Margaret Lockwood and the
possibility that hers is the first signature: 'To Anthony Best
wishes, Margaret Lockwood'. Lockwood was Peter Pan in 1949,
1950 and 1957. I can see myself now, with my father pulling
rank on the queue of children waiting for her autograph and
pushing to the front. That does not add up to a fifteen year old
boy, but it does add up to an eight year old. She was in four
other plays in the nineteen fifties, but I would not have been
taken to or gone to any of them. So it would seem as though
it was after a performance of the 1950 production of *Peter Pan*
– 1949 is too early – that I met her and got my first autograph.
As you would expect, every time I saw her autograph in the
album, my memory of the episode received a booster. Susannah
York appeared in *Peter Pan* in 1977, seven or eight years before
I became one of her theatre groupies, already alluded to in
my introduction. Paula has made wonderful images of this
story, which suits her up to the heavens (and her son Nicky
Willing's recent film is about J. M. Barrie). I surmised earlier
that Eddie Cantor's was my final autograph, dated March 1959.
Assuming I saw *Peter Pan* in the Christmas holidays of 1950
or in January 1951, my career as a collector lasted a little over
eight years. Later, as a publisher, I would use my contacts to
get autographs for my son Nathaniel. A signature, especially
if obtained in person, is a genuine relic, even more so than a
photograph, since the person is giving rather than taken. There
is an element of magic in autographs. No wonder they are sold
for high prices. The one which gives me the greatest frisson is
Kafka's in the private keepsake book of his school friend, the

philosopher and theologian Samuel Hugo Bergmann, born in the same year as Kafka, 1883 (private in the sense that it contained messages written for him, unlike the high school year book from *The Glass Menagerie*.) Bergmann showed it to me in his house in Rehavia, Jerusalem in 1969 and, indeed, allowed me to hold the book in my hands. I think it would have been inscribed in 1901 when they left school. The frisson is double: firstly, the message is from Kafka (whom I thus know at one remove, compare Shirley Eaton above). Secondly, he was not yet Kafka. I was looking at the handwriting of one who would only later become Kafka, a writer central to my life. There is some link here with my autograph of Alex Ehrlich whose earlier life meant nothing to me on the occasion we met. The Kafka circle turned full on itself when I posed naked for Paula as Gregor in her 'Metamorphosis', considered by Canetti to be Kafka's greatest work (see that masterpiece of close reading, *Kafka's Other Trial*).

The next page has had the lower half removed, for whatever reason. Upstairs is Max Bygraves – again, since I never met him, obtained for me by a third party. My earliest memory of his voice is his song 'You're a pink toothbrush, I'm a blue toothbrush . . . We met by the bathroom door', which was often heard on the Saturday morning Light Programme (later to transmogrify into Radio Two) request show *Children's Favourites* and which I would listen to before going to synagogue for the Children's Service. It was presented by Uncle Mac (of *Children's Hour* fame) and began: 'Hello children everywhere'. Until doing a spot of research today, I had forgotten that Bygraves was one of the tutors of the radio dummy Archie Andrews, in *Educating Archie*, although I listened to it regularly. On the other hand, I never forgot Max's catchphrases: 'I've arrived and to prove it I'm here' and 'It's a good idea [pause] son'. Other tutors were Tony Hancock, Benny Hill and Harry

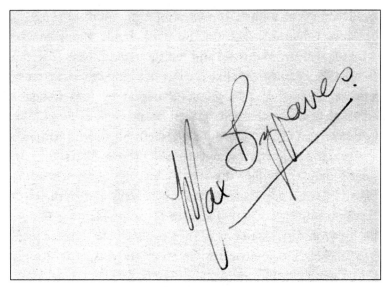

Max Bygraves

Secombe. A ventriloquist (Peter Brough) and his dummy on the wireless? Don't ask. When Beryl Reid as Archie's girlfriend said 'As the art mistress said to the gardener', I would not have been aware of the risqué connotation. On the next page we find 'Best wishes Elizabeth Allan' and 'Geoff Iden', whose signature survives incongruously amidst a bunch of show business ones. It was a close shave because against his name is an 'x' and the ominous word 'censor', i.e. remove, but I never got round to

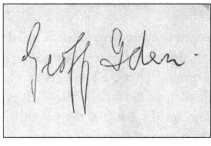

Geoff Iden

it. Iden was a marathon runner who came ninth in the 1952 Helsinki Olympics, famously won by Emile Zatopek after winning the five thousand and ten thousand metres. Zatopek (whose very name thuds like the feet of a long distance runner) was the subject of a biographical fiction by Jean Echenoz, although it is less compelling than his marvellous *Ravel*. Who knows where I met Iden, ditto Elizabeth Allan, who had been a film star but later appeared on panel shows like *What's My Line*. I only remember the regular line up: Gilbert Harding, David Nixon, Lady Barnet and Barbara Kelly and, in the chair, Eamonn Andrews. On one famous occasion, Harding, famous for his short fuse, asked one of the people whose jobs the panel had to guess: 'Do you require expertise?' and received the reply: 'No, I work alone'.

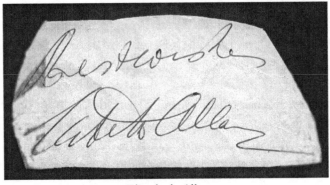

Elizabeth Allan

On the next page (apart from Ehrlich and Berzcik, all my signatures are on right-hand pages) we find 'for Anthony, Alma Cogan' and 'Sincerely Herbert Lom' (born Herbert Charles Angelo Cuchacevich ze Schluderpacheru). I am intrigued by the Lom because on the back of the proverbial envelope on which it is written are the following words:

H. C. Rudolf Esq.,
Messrs H. C. Rudolf & Company,
Balfour House.
London. E.C.2.

Why or where my father would have met Herbert Lom is now beyond resolution, unless I can ask the ninety-three year old Lom directly. Perhaps he was my father's client but the office files are doubtless destroyed or beyond my reach because of confidentiality, and there is no one left in the firm who would know. Of the four offices of my father that I remember – which were situated in Finsbury Square, Balfour House in Finsbury Pavement, City Road, Lee House off what is now the Barbican and Wilec House at Old Street Station (outside which he died of a heart attack in 1986) — Balfour House is my favourite. I wrote about it in *The Arithmetic of Memory*. My ex brother-in-law and quondam junior partner of my father, Alan Bell, tells me that the London Society of Accountants (now the Association of Chartered Certified Accountants) was founded in a room in Balfour House on November 30, 1904. My father's first office was a room in Tee & Whiten (printers), his first client and publisher of *Motor Sport* in Tabernacle Street. Like Lee House, Balfour House and Tee's building no longer exist. Malcolm Coleman, another retired partner, who remembers back to the Balfour House days, does not recall Herbert Lom. I have written to Lom, now aged ninety three, but do not expect a reply, even in the s.a.e. I enclosed for encouragement and out of courtesy.

Lom, famous for playing the winking Chief Inspector Dreyfus in *The Pink Panther* and Dracula, to name only two of his parts, has also written two books: on Christopher Marlowe and Doctor Guillotine. I asked my Czech friend Milos Vavra and his wife Mary Raine Vavrova about Lom's superb birth

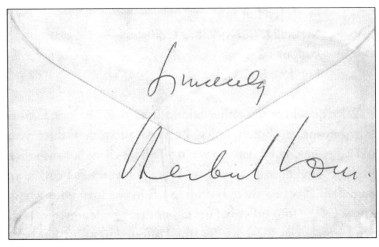

Herbert Lom

name: 'He was born in Prague in the days of the Austro-Hungarian empire. (That is how he came to have a Croatian or Slovene name, as many Czechs had links with that part of the world: they were good bureaucrats and worked in places like Dalmatia. There was a lot of inter-marriage). His family, though, came from the region of Sumava in Southern Bohemia bordering Austria and Germany) and young Lom spent a lot of time there as a boy. His grandfather was very minor nobility under the Hapsburgs (the title dates back to the early 1600s) and his family originated from Tyrol, "ze" being Czech for "von". Lom's father had a printing works and among other things printed theatre posters. The future actor studied at the country's top Arts department, the Charles University Philosophical Faculty. Understandably he decided to change his name and is said to have gone through the Prague telephone directory for inspiration. Lom (meaning "quarry") was the shortest he could find and liked best. Czech websites quote Lom as saying he thinks of himself as an Englishman now but has never forgotten or renounced his Czech roots and heritage. He may also be part Jewish. Despite his great age he apparently still speaks good Czech and follows events there with great interest.' *Coda at proof stage*: Herbert Lom died on September 27th 2012, preceded by Max Bygraves on 31st August.

The Autographs 4
Alma Cogan and Frankie Vaughan

I type into the search box of Spotify the words Alma Cogan and from the long list of songs choose to play 'Things aint what they used to be', written by Lionel Bart, one of whose cover dates she was. (Another lover of Cogan is said to have been John Lennon). Before the song starts, 'Miss Cogan' is asked by 'Bob', who is or sounds like a cockney doorman ('once in show business'), if she would sign his autograph book 'for my little grandson Tommy' and then they sing it as a duet. The wording in my own autograph book, 'For Anthony, Alma Cogan' suggests personal contact. But I never met her, although I remember going with my maternal grandmother, Rebecca Rosenberg, to see the hugely popular singer at the London Palladium. All the same, there was personal contact – at one remove. The autograph appears to be written on the back of a visiting card, which I have carefully removed from the ancient gluey page, thus ruining the pristine look of this and other pages, but the album is not necessarily a work of conceptual art. And, in the interests of truth and story, I had no choice. This is the visiting card of my uncle Leon Rudolf who, I would guess, met her at one of the (mainly) Jewish charities he supported, and probably did the printing for. The business which he ran with his brother Isadore – until the mother of all sibling quarrels — was called Radclyffe and Co ('for all your printing, stationery and office equipment')

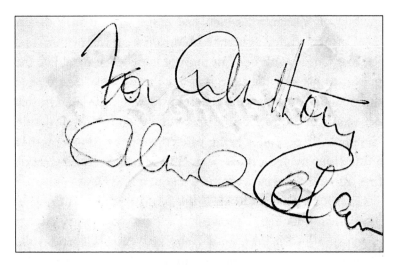

Alma Cogan

and was in Sun Street, Bishopsgate, between Henry Rudolf's office at Balfour House and Liverpool Street Station (phone BIShopsgate 4486, 'three lines'). I well remember regular visits when I was a child and, later, going there once or twice for lunch, always a version of eggs, cooked by my grandfather Josef Rudolf, one of his 'jobs' during the long post-retirement and widowerhood years. Uncles are important people: Isadore took me to football matches, Leon got me autographs. There was an interesting television programme about Cogan a few years ago, revealing how much the Beatles admired her, which prompts thoughts about the direction she would have taken had the nice Jewish girl – born while her parents, from the East End, were living in Golders Green – survived beyond the age of thirty four. (While I have not read Gordon Burn's novel *Alma Cogan*, which imagines that future, we can surmise from anecdotal evidence that she would have known how to adapt to the new world symbolised by the Beatles). It was on the piano at Cogan's flat that Paul McCartney first played the melody of 'Yesterday', which had come to him in a dream: 'McCartney wished assurance his dream song was original and felt that Cogan with her vast musical knowledge would be the person to identify the tune if it did already exist.' She replied that she didn't know what it was but it was beautiful. On that occasion, McCartney came up with the song's original title, 'Scrambled Eggs', after being offered some by Alma's mother, a title comparable in more ways than one to Scott Fitzgerald's first offering for what eventually became *The Great Gatsby*.

Given that Kogan/Cogan is the Russian way of spelling or pronouncing Cohen, I thought that hers was a witty change of name, a Jewish joke, until I checked 'Alma Cogan' in the *Dictionary of National Biography* and found her father named as Mark Cohen Cogan. Yet we find in *Alma Cogan*, the memoir by her actress singer Sandra Caron (whose surname was inspired by Lesley Caron's), that the family name was Kogin, which their father changed to Cogan, calling his shops Mark Cogan. Again, Caron tells us that Alma was very religious and always had a Bible with her, a gift from her father, and was distraught when she lost it. Alma Cogan died of ovarian cancer. After mentioning that definitive fact, an article in the *Jewish Chronicle* in 2006 on the fortieth anniversary of her death contains the cringe-making sentences: '. . . although or perhaps it was the 1960s which killed her. Her mother's line, "in the '60s, they forgot what sequins were for", was just perfect'. Whatever her mother's views on sequins, there are no grounds for thinking she agreed with the journalist's view that the sixties murdered the singer. On the morning after her death, the BBC played Alma singing 'Cheek to Cheek' which, of course, begins 'Heaven, I'm in heaven', an odd choice, perhaps, irrespective of the whereabouts of her posthumous destiny. The television film showed newsreel footage of people arriving at her funeral at Bushey Jewish cemetery, where my parents and Jon Silkin and Miron Grindea and so many other people I have known are buried. My grandparents Josef and Fanny Rudolf, however, are buried in Willesden Jewish cemetery, as is Uncle Leon's son, my cousin Derek Rudolf. Because he died before he was thirty days old, he is buried in a dedicated unmarked area for children of that age.

'When I first went to work on Mallorca, I watched Frankie Vaughan a number of times from the wings of a club called Titos (I knew the stage manager), in Palma's El Terreno, an area Graves described as an open pyschotic ward (he was at least half right). Fascinating to watch FV gear up for performance and then come off in a state of near collapse, only to recover himself instantly and go back on. Huge intensity, like a soldier in the frontline, perhaps. He never once questioned my presence there; we never spoke; and the show always went on', so writes my friend Bruce Ross Smith. On the next page of my album is a signed photograph of Frankie Vaughan, born Frankie Abelson. Unlike Alma Cogan's, his name change is a Jewish joke: his grandmother, with her Yiddish inflected Liverpool accent (and possibly inspired by Charlie Chan) called him her 'nomber von' grandson. Maria, Paula Rego's mother, pronounced the surname of one of her favourite writers, Evelyn Waugh, 'Vorgan', which brings 'Von' full circle and also chimes nicely with Cogan. (There is a blue plaque to Vorgan in Golders Green, of all places). The text on the back of the signed photograph refers to a 1955 ice-show which the former synagogue choir boy starred in, while 'The Green Door' topped the charts or the Hit Parade as it was known in 1957, which was when I would have listened to it in a booth at HMV's store in Oxford Street and when I would have written to his label Philips for an autograph. If I bought it, I no longer have it but playing it on Spotify reveals a good song sung well. I mentioned this song to my friend Clive Sinclair the other day as I was driving him and

Elaine Feinstein to the house in Chelsea where he lives with Haidee Becker. He said that on the corner of the very street we were in, Bramerton Street and Kings Road, was the eponymous lesbian nightclub which the songwriter was alluding to without Vaughan's knowledge. 'Green door, what's that secret you're keeping . . . Wish they'd let me in . . . Wonder what's going on in there . . . etc. etc'. Don't ask. The English words of his version of 'Milord' are cleverly rhymed. I would like to know who made the translation, perhaps it was Herbert Kretzmer.

I email Kretzmer via his agent and tell him I hope he will take it as a compliment that I thought the lyrics were good enough for him to have written them, but he sends a friendly reply in the negative. I then hit on the (obvious) idea of approaching the Performing Rights Society. The very helpful Nicola Formoy at the PRS consults their database and comes up with the name of the publishers of the song. A swift phone call to Carlin Music reveals that the lyrics writer was Bunny Lewis. Lewis, who died in 2001, co-composed 'Cara Mia', which I am listening to in Mantovani's version on Spotify. Then there is 'My Boy Flat Top'. What a weird song, and Vaughan sings it without conviction, flatly. Frankie Vaughan had a social conscience, working with tough boys in Glasgow housing estates, negotiating a truce between two gangs, and getting them to give up their guns. He lived not far from me and had the same NHS doctor, who was not over-impressed by his taste in wallpaper. On *Yom Kippur* every year at Woodside Park Synagogue Vaughan participated in the reading of the Book of Jonah. He was not swallowed up by Marilyn Monroe when in Hollywood. There are two versions of the story: one is that he decided alone not to accept an invitation to her apartment to read their parts together, the other is that his wife told him that MM's intentions went beyond the professional (i.e. involved a different pair of parts) and that he mustn't go.

PHILIPS *The Records of the Century*

Frankie Vaughan

My Golders Green barber Johnny used to be in Macclesfield Street, Soho, where I first found him on my return from the USA in 1966. In the early days of Macclesfield Street, the shop was open plan, upstairs the ladies department run by Johnny's brother Gaye, downstairs the gents. In the basement was Katie, turning her tricks. In those days Frankie and Stella Vaughan had a flat across the road. A few years later, Frank was in Johnny's for a haircut when he noticed Katie upstairs having her hair done by Gaye. 'Good heavens, is that Katie? Stella and I haven't seen her for years.' He dashed upstairs and gave her a hug. Some years later again, when the ladies department had moved to Edgware Road, Katie went upstairs from the Macclesfield Street basement and asked Johnny for a haircut. He reminded her that he only did gents, but she replied don't be daft, all she wanted was a trim, and raised her skirt.

Like Alma, Frankie is buried at Bushey, and I shall visit his and Alma's graves next time I go there to visit my father's (now my mother's too). In fact, only a few days after writing those words, I found myself at Bushey for the funeral of Yasha Krom, the father of my sister Mary's husband Mike. This was during the big freeze just before Christmas 2010. I arrived half an hour early and obtained the grave addresses from the office. When I reached the blocks (the two singers are buried very close to each other), I could not identify the exact rows because of the snow, and then found myself, appropriately enough, in front of the graves of Clive Sinclair's parents. I phoned him at once. Unfortunately he was unable to direct me, and I shall have to wait for another funeral or go there on a dedicated visit after the bad weather.

Coda: June 12, 2011: I drove to Bushey Jewish cemetery, about twenty five minutes from where I live, for two reasons: firstly, to show my daughter Naomi and grandson Charlie the double grave of my mother and father and secondly, to revisit, only yards away, Alma's tomb. After Charlie placed a painted stone on the grave of, in his words, 'great grandma Esther', we walked to the hedge which bisects the cemetery and found Alma's grave a little further on: H–1–12, that is, grave number 12 in row 1 of H-block. This sounds like a prison and, indeed, once admitted, no one leaves here, until amnesty on the Day of Judgment. Some of the lyrics of 'Hernando's Hideaway', another famous song about a night club (see 'Green Door' earlier) and which Alma recorded the year before she died, are uncannily relevant to a cemetery.

The tomb itself: the English letters ALMA are carved at the top of the vertical stone. In Ashkenazi Jewish cemeteries vertical stones are traditional practice. Should you ever visit Golders Green crematorium, cross the road to the Jewish cemetery, where you can see vertical tombstones to the left and, in the Sephardi section on the right, horizontal ones. Below the word ALMA, reading from right to left, are the Hebrew letters פ and ט, initials of the two words in a formulaic phrase 'Po tamuna', 'Here lies hidden'. The next line contains her Hebrew name, beginning with the abbreviated word (note the apostrophe) 'ה ב ת, the first three letters of the word 'Habetulah', meaning the spinster or the virgin or, in this context, the young woman or the unmarried woman. No one I have consulted has ever seen the word 'Habetulah' on a tombstone and one is curious as to who advised Alma's mother about the wording. (Was it the 'revered rabbi' Alma's mother and sister visited while Alma was in hospital, as revealed in her sister's memoir?). The word is, however, found on orthodox 'ketuboth' (marriage certificates), meaning virgin or unmarried woman, which are or were virtually synonymous. This is rich territory for Christian theology, with centuries of debate about the status of 'the virgin' Mary, based on the meaning of the Hebrew words 'betulah' and (appropriately enough) 'alma'. In modern Israel,

IN TREASURED AND UNFORGETTABLE
MEMORIES OF A MOST WONDERFUL
AND ADORED DAUGHTER

ALMA COGAN

WHO PASSED AWAY
26TH OCTOBER 1966.

SHE WAS MORE PRECIOUS THAN
RUBIES AND ALL THE THINGS
THOU CANST DESIRE WERE NOT
TO BE COMPARED WITH HER.

WHILST LIFE AND MEMORY LASTS
WE WILL REMEMBER.

OH FOR THE TOUCH OF
A VANISHED HAND AND FOR
THE SOUND OF A VOICE THAT
IS STILLED.

DEEPLY LOVED AND SO GREATLY
MISSED BY HER MOTHER
SISTER AND BROTHER
ALSO SISTER-IN-LAW, NEPHEW
NIECE, AUNTS AND UNCLES
GREAT-AUNTS, GREAT-UNCLES
RELATIVES AND A LARGE
CIRCLE OF DEAR FRIENDS.

REST IN PEACE MY DARLING.

Below this, on the horizontal stone, we find a plaque:

IN EVER LOVING MEMORY OF
DEAR ALMA
FROM HER DEVOTED FANS

the word for a young woman is 'bachara' or, less commonly, 'alma'. No doubt Alma's parents had in mind the traditional English name Alma which means nourishing, as in alma mater. Back to the tombstone: after 'Habet', we find 'Chaya bat R[eb] Mordecai', Chaya daughter of ['Reb' is a Yiddish honorific from the word for rabbi but it does not mean rabbi] the honoured Mordecai, Mordecai being her father Mark's Hebrew name. It is common enough for Jewish parents to choose an English name beginning with the same letter as the Hebrew name. The next line of the Hebrew contains the date: 'died on the 12th of Marcheshvan, 5727. The last line consists of the traditional acronym .ת.נ.צ.ב.ה. 'May her soul be bound up in the bond of life.' (see First Samuel 25:29). 'Marcheshvan' is another name for 'Cheshvan' and means 'bitter Cheshvan', so called because

there are no festivals in the month but chosen for this tomb-stone for the obvious reason. And from her music director, Stan Foster, since deceased, the words in the illustration on the opposite page. Also, as is traditional, some pebbles left by unknown people as well as one with a hand-written message:

Dear A, always in my thoughts, Stan

The long inscription was clearly written in high emotion and left me strangely elated because I chose the title of this book some weeks ago, before finding it on the tombstone during this, my final piece of research. The first two lines of the inscription conflate two thoughts: 'In' requires 'memory' or 'memories' requires 'with'. At first I thought Alma's mother had misquoted Proverbs 3.15 (English inscription lines 7–10) but now I think she has deliberately put it in the past tense.

And while the quote from Tennyson (lines 13–17) contains an unintended error (the second 'for' should not be there), what I originally thought was an error in line 16 ('stilled' where Tennyson wrote 'still') I now reckon is an angry and legitimate reinforcement, given that the singer's voice is not merely still but was 'stilled' while in her prime.

Twenty or thirty yards from Alma, Frankie Vaughan is buried in ZG-8-5. At the top of his tombstone is his Hebrew name which, transliterated from the original, reads: Ephraim Chaim (life, cf Alma's name Chaya, female version of the same name, like Vitus and Vita in Latin, I suppose) ben Yitzhak Halevi, that is son of Isaac the Levite. Descent from the priestly Levites and Cohens runs through the male line, so Frankie Vaughan, like my maternal grandfather, was a Levite.

FRANK VAUGHAN C.B.E., D.L.

3.2.1928 – 17.9.1999

LOVINGLY REMEMBERED BY

HIS WIFE STELLA

CHILDREN DAVID SUSAN AND ANDREW

GRANDCHILDREN, SISTERS

FAMILY AND FRIENDS

MR MOONLIGHT

HE ENRICHED OUR LIVES

On the horizontal stone is a plaque:

We will	Natalie
always	Lillie
miss	Jamie
our darling	and
grandpa	Annabelle

פ"נ
אפרים חיים בן יצחק הלוי ז"ל

FRANK VAUGHAN C.B.E. D.L.

3. 2. 1928 - 17. 9. 1999

LOVINGLY REMEMBERED BY
HIS WIFE STELLA
CHILDREN DAVID, SUSAN AND ANDREW,
GRANDCHILDREN, SISTERS,
FAMILY AND FRIENDS.

MR MOONLIGHT
HE ENRICHED OUR LIVES

ת נ צ ב ה

The Autographs (5)

More cricketers on the next page: Jack Robertson's signature has been cut out of a scorecard. Pasted onto a pink card which itself is pasted onto a white card, in turn pasted onto the page. The rationale for this technique, if there was one, is irretrievable. Jack Robertson was one of the best opening bats in the country who nonetheless only played for England eleven times, mainly because during his time England had a settled opening pair, Hutton and Washbrook. I rooted for Robertson because he played for Middlesex, the county I supported, a county which survives in cricket despite having been abolished as a political and administrative entity. His 331 remains the highest ever score for Middlesex. Below Robertson are five signatures on a white card, Sussex and Middlesex players, so we know who was playing on the day I got the autographs. The venue would have been Lords since I never saw a county match in Sussex. Three of the five are Sussex players. One is a Middlesex player, John Warr, whom I have already mentioned. He later became President of the MCC. Sadly, he had the worst average of any English test bowler, playing in only two test matches – in 1951–2 – and taking one wicket for 281. The Sussex players are: Alan Oakman, who played for England twice (in 1956), I. Thomson (who played in five tests in 1964/5), and Jim Parks, who played forty six times for England, all in the nineteen sixties from 1964, except his first which was in 1954 and was presumably a disaster, leading to his being dropped for ten years. The fifth is illegible, and no amount of reading it against the names of Middlesex and Sussex players online generates a solution. Perhaps it was an umpire. An e-mail appeal to my school contemporay Mike Brearley sadly fails: he cannot decipher them either.

A whole bunch of footballers come next, beginning with a signed photograph of the the well-loved inside-forward Jimmy Logie, for which I presumably wrote off to the Arsenal, quite likely enclosing a stamped addressed envelope. Despite being highly regarded, he played only once for his native Scotland. Wikipedia says he ended up working as a newsagent in Piccadilly Circus but I recall a press report that he was selling papers outside Leicester Square tube station, half a mile away. There is a suggestion that he gambled away the little money players of that generation earned; all the same, one can guess what he thought of George Best. Against his photograph I have written 'censor' which is very strange, since I have not written it against the signature of another Arsenal player of the fifties, the Welsh international and manager Dave Bowen on the next page, a player who showed up far less on my personal radar. These signatures, plus those of less successful players such as Joe Wade (he too stigmatised with the mark of the 'censor') and Don Bennett, I recall obtaining on a visit to

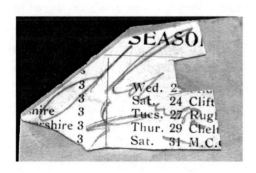

Jack Robertson

from left to right: unidentified, Jim Parks, A. Oakman,
I. Thomson, John Warr

a training session at Highbury, probably in 1955. Don Bennett also played cricket for Middlesex but his signature is here amidst the soccer players so, yes, he would have been among the soccer players I met on that visit to Highbury, along with Tommy Lawton, a very big name, whose career like so many was broken by the war and who played for Arsenal for two years from 1953. Unlike Joe Wade, there is no 'censor' against Lawton's name. I was making a virtue out of necessity by going to Highbury, the nearest club to my home. The team I supported was Wolverhampton Wanderers – perhaps because they were the First Division champions in 1953–4, perhaps because their captain, Billy Wright, was England's captain, but, to be fair, I remember liking the club's name, which was the reason I backed Royal Tan in the 1954 Grand National, and duly won a bet with my father. I recall a parody of 'My old man's a dustman': 'My old man's a dustman he wears a dustman's hat, he bought a two bob ticket to see a football match. The ball was in the centre, the ha'penny whistle blew, fatty passed to skinny and down the wing he flew. Fatty passed

Jimmy Logie

to skinny, skinny passed to fat, fatty took a deep breath and knocked the goalie flat. Where was the goalie while the ball was in the net? Hanging from the goalpost with his trousers round his neck. Singing we can kick 'em, we can pass, we can kick 'em up the Arse . . . nal'. Over to Spotify to listen to Lonnie Donegan's personalised version of the real thing.

Here is a special page, pasted into the album: the torn off cover of the Arsenal versus Manchester United programme for their match on Saturday April 23, 1955. Seated in the row behind Uncle Isadore and myself was Leslie Compton, retired from playing but still working at the Gunners as a coach and scout. Older brother of my great hero, Denis Compton, Leslie played soccer for the Arsenal for twenty-two years and cricket for Middlesex for eighteen years. In 1955 he was still

Dave Bowen

Don Bennett

Joe Wade

Tommy Lawton

Middlesex's wicket-keeper, albeit on the brink of handing the gloves over to John Murray. I was always pleased for Leslie, who in many respects was in the shade of Denis, that he was a full England soccer international (twice, in 1950, aged 38) whereas Denis only played in a War international, which did not count in the record books. Leslie did not play cricket for England. According to Wisden (with one of its rare references to sports other than cricket), he became England's and remains England's oldest soccer debutant. Given the modern cult of youth and fitness, it is a safe bet that this achievement will remain in the record books for ever. In 1947–48, Les and Denis created a fraternal record: playing in a County Championship-winning side in the summer and in the First Division champion football team the following winter. Les Compton, after retiring from sport, ran a pub on Highgate Hill. My friend Bob Trevor, old World Service sports journalist, former President of the NUJ and author of a charming memoir *Blitz Boy*, reckons it was the Angel. The local historical society doesn't know, nor does the unofficial Middlesex historian, name and address supplied by Lords.

In *The Arithmetic of Memory*, I wrote that Billy Wright was my winter hero, Denis Compton my summer hero. Wearing my own eternal tracksuit, I once saw Billy, also in a tracksuit, outside Waitrose in Whetstone, where he lived with his Beverley Sister wife, Joy. The Spice Girls the Sisters weren't, although it is just possible Emma Bunton's father delivered letters to Wright. On the reverse of Billy's signed photograph is a message from Lucozade saying that they own the copyright in the photo and we are also told that 'the sparkling glucose drink replaces lost energy'. I remember buying dextrosol tablets for energy from the chemists shop Hugh Lloyds in Market Place, not Dexedrine as I wrongly called it in *The Arithmetic of Memory*. I did not like the taste of Lucozade, formerly known as Glucozade.

Apparently one 500ml bottle contains twenty one teaspoons of sugar. Sports sponsorship has been around longer than one realised, albeit using the fame of only a few famous players, such as Reg Harris, Billy Wright and the Brylcreem players. Stanley Matthews, vegetarian and teetotal, was paid to sponsor Craven 'A' cigarettes, which was a favourite brand among the working classes (just as Gary Lineker would advertise potato crisps forty years later).

As already stated, I had a collection of cigarette cards (which to my everlasting regret I gave away to a friend) but I did not realise that they were a form of advertising. Smokers like my father would give the cards in each packet to their sons, who with any luck would in turn become smokers. Stanley Matthews' great rival and partner as an England winger Tom Finney of Preston North End, like many top players, had a day job. He was a plumber. The Centre for the Sociology of Sport quotes one authority (Russell, 1997, but not listed in the online bibliography) as saying: 'Tom Finney's last match at Preston in 1961 signalled the end of an era in which supporters and players shared local attachments and broadly similar lifestyles'. Stuck onto the album page after Billy Wright is a page torn from somewhere else: 'To Anthony, with best wishes, Billy Steel'. Steel was a Scottish international forward who played for Dundee and ended his career as a precursor of David Beckham in Los Angeles. The flyleaf page was torn from Steel's autobiography although heaven knows which person, doubtless one of my father's clients, gave me the book. Against the page, I have written: 'Censor (put back in book)'. I recall that I tore it out of the book in the first place because you wanted to show off autographs to friends and could not very well take the book along with the album wherever you went. Evidently I later felt some remorse at removing the flyleaf from the book. However, it remains in the album, doubtless because I lost interest in

Leslie Compton

collecting autographs at a certain point and abandoned ship.

A cricket scorecard pasted into my album, which I have successfully unpasted to read the reverse side, is rich with possibility, although I no longer remember whom I went with to the second day of the final Ashes test of 1956, held at the Oval. Doubtless I did not go to the Lords test because, unlike the Oval, it was in term time. Possibly my companion was Paul Rochman, definitely not Michael Pinto-Duschinsky who had a skin condition preventing him from being in the sun. I wonder

Billy Wright

if the former Prime Minister, John Major, later president of the club, was there as a schoolboy. Born in March 1943, he is six months younger than me. Evidently Major and I look or looked alike because, while he was Prime Minister, I was quite often stopped in the street: 'Are you the Prime Minister?', asked some schoolboys. 'Would I be walking around North Finchley in a tracksuit if I was John Major?' My nearest and dearest could not see it, but I could, and all those strangers thought so too. Vox populi, or what. The cricket gave me an excuse to write to him about our physical resemblance. I told him about the schoolboys, enclosed a photograph of me, and also a photocopy of the score card. Eventually a reply came from his Chief of Staff, Arabella Warburton: John Major did attend the test match on the first day, when Compton played his last test innings.

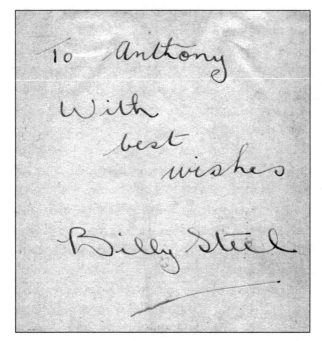

Billy Steel

There was no comment from him on the alleged likeness and she herself saw none.

Hugh Tayfield and Crawford White, the two signatures on my score card: my old Cambridge friend John Barrell did not need the following explanation when I consulted him, though non cricket fans or cricket non fans among my readers should be informed that Hugh Tayfield was a famous and distinguished South African off-spin bowler. All the same, I am not sure that it wasn't Crawford White whom I recognised first. He was the cricket correspondent of the *News Chronicle* which we took at home along with *The Times* and it is possible his photograph was printed alongside his by-line. According to the *Guardian* obituary of White in 2000, 'his most difficult job was ghosting Denis Compton's column'. The previous test at Old Trafford saw Laker take nineteen wickets (eat your heart out, rival Tayfield), a unique record to this day. I consulted John because I wasn't sure if I attended the Oval on the first or second day, and accuracy, as in left arm spin bowling, is of the essence. At first I thought that I picked up the scorecard – which shows England all out for 247 and Australia 13 for three wickets – at the end of play on the first day but John Barrell writes, consulting his memory and the 1957 Wisden which he owns: 'if memory serves, Compton was out for 94 after six o'clock on the first day, and, in failing light, May decided to send in Lock as night-watchman. But he was out first ball to Archer, and so Washbrook had to come in. He averted the hat-trick but fell before the close, also to Archer; Evans immediately fell to Miller, and England ended the day at 223 for 7, having been 222–3 half an hour before.' The score on my card suggests that the printers on the ground were late in bringing it out on the second morning or, less likely, brought out a second edition quickly. I remember we had our own score books on whose blank templates we could keep score, but mine have not survived the passing of time.

Cyril Washbrook was aged forty-one and was one of the England selectors. The first four England batsmen on the scorecard are listed as P. E. Richardson, M. C. Cowdrey, Rev. D. S. Shepherd (later Anglican Bishop of Liverpool) and P. B. H. May. The rest of the England team was Compton, D. C. S., Lock, G. A. R., Evans T. G. (keeping wicket of course), Laker J. C., Tyson F. H., and Statham, J. B. Note the initials: the first four England players were amateurs ('Gentlemen'), the last seven professionals ('Players') and the convention, which I touched on earlier in respect of John Warr, was to identify them by the position of their initials. On the other hand the entire Australian team have their initials first. John Barrell explains: 'all the Australians were adjudged to be amateurs in those days. If memory serves, and it does, there were only five teams in the Sheffield Shield at that time, too few to justify their paying professionals, and they played only over long weekends, but not on Sundays.' The match was eventually drawn. England won the rubber and the Ashes. Barrell very kindly scanned the Wisden match report for me. The scorecard cost me three old pence, has its own individual number 171011 (or is that the number of the edition?) and an advertisement for 'Shell with ICA': 'Only Shell has both high octane and I.C.A'. I emailed Shell's customer service to find out what ICA stands for and received no reply. Perhaps they think I am an anti-pollution activist. Odd how John Barrell was the only person I could turn to, given that a few weeks earlier I asked him if he could tell me the name of the anonymous author of an 1816 article in the *Edinburgh Review*.

(*Coda*: a recent obituary of the Middlesex off-spinner Fred Titmus refers to a loudspeaker announcement at Lords con-

... *but you can be sure of*

SHELL WITH **ICA**

ONLY SHELL HAS BOTH HIGH OCTANE AND I.C.A

FIXTURES AT THE OVAL 1956

S	MAY	5, 7, 8	DERBYSHIRE
W	,,	9,10,11	NORTHAMPTONSHIRE
W	,,	16,17,18	AUSTRALIANS
W	,,	30,31, 1	LEICESTERSHIRE
S	JUNE	2, 4, 5	SOMERSET
Th	,,	7, 8	A SURREY XI v SURREY ASSOC. OF CRICKET CLUBS
S	,,	16,18,19	YORKSHIRE (Benefit Match for J. C. Laker)
W	,,	20,21,22	OXFORD U.
S	,,	30, 2, 3	KENT
W	JULY	11,12,13	GLOUCESTERSHIRE
S	,,	14,16,17	COMBINED SERVICES
F	,,	20	AUSTRALIANS v CLUB CRICKET C.

S	JULY	21,23	Women's Cricket Assoc.— Home Counties v The Rest
S	,,	28,30,31	ESSEX
W	AUG.	1, 2, 3	AUSTRALIANS
S	,,	4, 6, 7	NOTTINGHAMSHIRE
S	,,	11,13,14	MIDDLESEX
W	,,	15,16,17	SUSSEX

Commencing on

Th	AUG.	23 — 28	ENGLAND v AUSTRALIA
W	,,	29,30,31	LANCASHIRE
W	SEPT.	5, 6, 7	WARWICKSHIRE
S	,,	8 — 12	CHAMPION COUNTY v REST OF ENGLAND

№ 171011

Hugh Tayfield and Crawford White

Surrey County Cricket Club 3ᴰ·

KENNINGTON OVAL

ENGLAND v. AUSTRALIA

Thursday, August 23rd, 1956 (5 Day Match)

ENGLAND	First Innings		Second Innings
1 P. E. Richardson ....Worcestershire	c Langley, b Miller	37	
2 M. C. Cowdrey ....Kent	c Langley, b Lindwall	0	
3 Rev. D. S. Sheppard ......Sussex	c Archer, b Miller	24	
*4 P. B. H. May ....Surrey	not out	83	
5 Compton, D. C. S.......Middlesex	c Davidson, b Archer	94	
10 Lock, G. A. R................Surrey	c Langley, b Archer	0	
6 Washbrook, C. ......Lancashire	lbw b Archer	0	
‡7 Evans, T. G. ....Kent	lbw b Miller	0	
8 Laker, J. C. ....Surrey	c Archer, b Miller	4	
9 Tyson, F. H. Northamptonshire	c Davidson, b Archer	3	
11 Statham, J. B..........Lancashire	b Archer	0	
	B , l-b , w2 , n-b	2	B , l-b , w , n-b
	Total..........	247	Total..........

FALL OF THE WICKETS

1—1	2—53	3—66	4—222	5—222	6—222	7—223	8—231	9—243	10—247
1—	2—	3—	4—	5—	6—	7—	8—	9—	10—

BOWLING ANALYSIS	First Innings						Second Innings				
	O.	M.	R.	W.	Wd.	N.b.	O.	M.	R.	W.	Wd.	N.b
Lindwall...........	18	5	36	1								
Miller	40	7	91	4	2							
Davidson	5	1	16	0								
Archer..............	28.2	7	53	5								
Johnson	9	2	28	0								
Benaud	9	2	21	0								

NEW BALL. The NEW BALL may be taken at the discretion of the fielding captain either (a) after 200 runs have been scored or (b) after 75 overs have been bowled. In the latter case a WHITE disc will be shown on the main score board at the end of the 65th over and will be replaced by a YELLOW disc after the 70th over. At the commencement of the 75th over both discs will be exposed and remain until the new ball has been taken.

NEXT MATCH AT THE OVAL, WED., AUGUST 29th (3 Day Match) SURREY v. LANCASHIRE

AUSTRALIA	First Innings		Second Innings
1 C. C. McDonald ....Victoria	c Lock, b Tyson	3	
2 J. W. Burke ....New South Wales	b Laker	8	
3 R. N. Harvey................Victoria			
4 I. D. Craig ...New South Wales	c Statham, b Lock	2	
*10 I. W. Johnson ....Victoria			
5 K. R. Miller ....New South Wales			
6 R. G. Archer ....Queensland			
7 R. Benaud.......New South Wales			
8 A. K. Davidson New South Wales			
9 R. R. Lindwall ....Queensland			
‡11 G. R. Langley ....South Australia			
	B , l-b , w , n-b		B , l-b , w , n-b
	Total..........		Total..........

FALL OF THE WICKETS

1—3	2—17	3—20	4—	5—	6—	7—	8—	9—	10—
1—	2—	3—	4—	5—	6—	7—	8—	9—	10—

BOWLING ANALYSIS	First Innings						Second Innings				
	O.	M.	R.	W.	Wd.	N.b.	O.	M.	R.	W.	Wd.	N.b.

*Captain   ‡Wkt.-keeper   Toss won by—ENGLAND
Umpires—Davies, D. & Bartley, T. J.   RESULT—

HOURS OF PLAY—ALL DAYS—11.30—6.30   Lunch 1.30

Printed on the ground by the Surrey County Cricket Club Printing Department

The Autographs (5) ✧ 71

cerning the scorecard: 'For F. J. Titmus please read Titmus F. J.'. Apart from calypsos ('those two little pals of mine / Ramadhin and Valentine', the chorus to the victory calypso of 1950), the only song that I know of which refers to cricket is on an album called *Back in the DHSS*, made by the Indie group Half Man Half Biscuit, 'Fuckin' 'ell, it's Fred Titmus'. I never met him to obtain his autograph; nor did the lead singer meet him.

Immediately after these cricketers and soccer players we come to three, possibly four, radio and/or television personalities: first a signed photograph of the sports commentator Kenneth Wolstenholme, famous the length and breadth of the national football mind for 'They think it's all over . . . It is now' after England won the 1966 world cup at Wembley, the very words on the faces of Prince William and David Beckham after England lost the 2018 world cup bid recently. Odd that no commentator, at least none that I saw, thought of the perfect reprise. The photograph of Wolstenholme is followed, on pieces of paper pasted in from another notebook, by the signatures of Wilfrid Thomas on one and, on the second, Sylvia Peters and an illegible less extravert signature which is clarified in the light of the wikipedia entry on Peters: it is that of her husband Kenneth Milne-Buckley, a television director, whom I would not have recognised but who must have been with her when I obtained the autographs. Peters herself was one of the first television presenters. She hosted the Queen's coronation in 1953 and retired aged thirty two in 1958, inaugurating a tradition of early retirement for female presenters that survives to this day, with this difference, that these days the tradition is publicly resented and contested by the victims. Wilfrid Thomas was an Australian-born radio broadcaster, whose details I can live without.

Kenneth Wolstenholme

Wilfrid Thomas

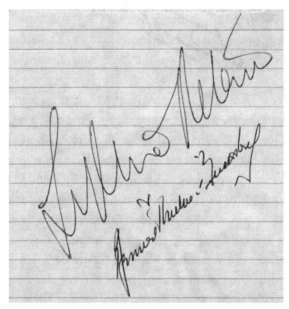

Sylvia Peters and Kenneth Milne-Buckley

Pièce de Résistance

The *pièce de résistance* in my album is a four-page programme and menu, folded in and secured by a rubber band rather than risk damage to the document. It marks an event at the National Sporting Club on Tuesday 18th September, 1956, which took place at the Club Headquarters, The Cafe Royal (no é) W.1. This, to quote from the front page, was 'a Dinner & Presentation to Honour Mr. Stanley Matthews on the occasion of his Silver Jubilee in Professional Football, 1931-1956.' Bottom right, there is a cut-out photo of 'Stanley Matthews N.S.C 1956' against a drawn corner flag and, top left, in a drawn ring, one of 'Jack Matthews N.S.C 1912', Stanley's father who, according to a note on the back page, fought at the old club in Covent Garden. Stanley Matthews was forty one years old the year of the dinner, and still playing at an international level, unthinkable today (except maybe in goal), even at club level (where he played until fifty). Reading the note, which summarises Stanley's career, we are told he won seventy six England caps, yet the record books say fifty four. Maybe the NSC included his wartime internationals minus some disputed ones. The maths almost adds up. Even so, there is a general point to be made about the interruption of great careers begun before the war, such as Denis Compton's, but the most dramatic interruption remains that of the Auschwitz-survivor, Alex Ehrlich: some interruption. Also on the back cover is a list of the committee members of the National Sporting Club, with some names still recognizable to people of my generation: Billy Butlin, Donald Campbell, Charles Forte (owner of the Café Royal), Hector Hughes MP, Alfred Robens MP. But the others I shall check out in the *Dictionary of National Biography* and *Who's Who* and other reference sites I can access through Google. Perhaps a few details will be of interest:

Item: Lieutenant-Colonel M.W. Batchelor, JP, was mentioned in dispatches.

Item: Sir James Carreras, MBE, was Chairman of Hammer Films and executive producer of the Dick Barton films, and many others.

Item: C.B. Follett esq. No mention.

Item: John E. Harding esq. No mention.

Item: Sir Leslie Joseph was vice-chairman of Fortes.

Item: Lieutenant Colonel W. H. Kingsmill, DSO, MC, was a property developer.

Item: C. J. Lytle. No mention.

Item: Sir Alexander Maxwell KCMG. Retired permanent under-secretary at the Home Office, including during World War Two. As such, he was heavily involved in policy concerning the imprisonment of enemy aliens, and at all times the prerogative of mercy for condemned persons and so on. According to the *Dictionary of National Biography*, 'It was so like Maxwell that he and his wife, with their two sons as waiters, should give annual parties at Toynbee Hall for the Home Office charladies, all of whom, it was said, he knew by their first names . . . A valuable committee man, he presided in 1936 over the inquiry into the work of Metro-politan Police courts and in 1949 he was a member of the royal commission on capital punishment.' I would guess that, like the hangman himself Albert Pierrepoint (after his moonlighting job had been abolished), Maxwell came out against capital punishment.

Item: The Earl of Midleton (not the Earl of Middleton), served in World War I, 1914–17 (Legion of Honour, MC) and World War II, 1939-45 (ADC to C-in-C Home Forces)

Item: Marquess of Queensberry. The 11th Marquess. The 9th, his grandfather, was patron of the boxing rules named after him and, as the father of Lord Alfred Douglas, is even more famous for the litigation against Oscar Wilde.

Item: Lieutenant-Colonel R.S. Rogers. No mention.

Item: Lord Selsdon, DSC. Racing driver who co-drove the winner of the 1949 Le Mans.

Item: Rear-Admiral Tully Shelley, CBE. The year after the dinner, Shelley, 'managing director of a company of oil refinery and construction engineers, designed a match striking machine as an April Fool's Day joke. He called it his 'Yonghy Bonghy Bo.' However, the machine actually did work and could be used to light a cigarette'. The title was taken from a poem by Edward Lear.

Item: Charles Sweeney. No mention.

Item: Sir Louis Sterling. The future industrialist was born into a poor Jewish family in New York in 1879. He emigrated to Europe in 1903. A pioneer in the burgeoning record industry, he sold his own business to Columbia records which he then joined as British sales manager on a commission basis only. Talk about self-confidence! By 1917 he was managing director of the European branch of the company and initiated research which would lead to major improvements in the quality of recorded sound. 'By the early 1930s he had integrated much of the world's record industry and was a major electrical goods manufacturer'. He became deeply involved in the development of television – the BBC at Alexandra Palace used EMI technology. Although he was a multi-millionaire, he never abandoned his early progressive views and was a member of the Labour Party at a time when the party leadership was not 'intensely relaxed about people getting filthy rich as long as they pay their taxes', to coin a phrase. In 1929, on his fiftieth birthday, he distributed £100,000 (four million pounds in today's money) of his personal wealth among Columbia employees and, what's more, established and endowed a company pension scheme. In 1931, as a result of a merger, he became Managing Director of a new company, EMI, which he left after a disagreement with the chairman in 1937. In 1938, this 'luminary' became a founding partner of S. G. Warburg, the merchant bank founded by a more recent arrival on these shores. Knighted in 1937, Sterling and his wife held a regular Sunday afternoon salon at 7 Avenue Road, almost at Regents Park. No 7 is now a block of flats. At one of these gatherings, according to an article in *The Gramophone*, 'Schnabel and Kreisler were deeply engrossed in discussing the political situation in Germany and were joined by ex-Mayor of New York Jimmy Walker and the great tenor Lauritz Melchior, greatly to the discomfort of a bridge party in the next room, which included Chaliapin and Gigli'. Sterling was a major league philanthropist who endowed the library in Senate House, which houses his fabulous collection of first editions and bears his name (see *TLS* February 4, 1939 for details). He died in 1958 and is buried in Willesden Jewish cemetery, like my grandfather, who was born one year after him but survived many more years. Sir Louis Sterling is a very interesting figure, certainly the most interesting one on the NSC committee. Perhaps he deserves a biography, although he is not as significant as, say, Siegmund Warburg. I was dipping into Jacques Attali's book on Warburg and found only one reference to Sterling, namely that he was one of the five people employed by Warburg in 1935, two years after the banker arrived in London. This seems unlikely given, as I wrote above, that he was head of EMI at the time and, apparently, become a founding partner at Warburg's later on. Attali did not answer my email requesting clarification. Either his secretary did not forward it or I'm right on this point and he's not about to admit it. Either way, I'm not in the least bit qualified to write Sterling's biography. There is only one person whose biography I have ever wanted to write, and that is Léon Blum.

On the left of the inside pages of the programme is the list of Speakers following 'The Loyal Toast'. They are

Mr Charles Forte
(Chairman: National Sporting Club Committee)

Sir Stanley Rouse, CBE, JP
(Secretary of the Football Association)

Tommy Trinder, Esq

Billy Wright, Esq
(Captain of England and
Wolverhampton Wanderers Football Club)

Rt. Hon. The Lord Mancroft, MBE, TD
(Under-Secretary of State for Home Affairs)

Stanley Matthews, Esq

On the right is the menu:

Bisques de Crevettes

. . .

Turbot poche Belonaise

. . .

Selle d'Agneau
Haricots Verts au Beurre
Pommes Fondantes

. . .

Peches farcies Chatelaine
Rocher Vanille

. . .

Cafe

No wine is listed, which surely was not because the teetotal
Matthews influenced the menu. The *DNB* speaks of 'his diet
of carrot juice at lunchtime and steak and salad for dinner. He
fasted every Monday'. Eric Cantona might object to the lack
of accents in the menu-French (can you spot them?), and in
this respect the list nerd in me is saddled (agneau-like) with
the French nerd. Much more important than the menu are the
autographs scribbled around it. To the left: 'To Anthony from
Uncle Leon Rudolf', to the right: Mike Hawthorn, Tommy
Trinder, Peter Dimmock, James Seed, J. C. Laker (compare
the cricket programme), S. Matthews and Denis Compton
(the last named 'a likeable rogue . . . who claimed expenses for
an item he classified as 'miscellaneous' . . . The FA official in
question told Denis 'You don't even know how to spell it.'*
Bless Uncle Leon for this septet, especially for my summer
hero, Denis Compton. What was Leon doing at the dinner?
My hunch is that he printed the programme for free and was
invited to the dinner as a thank you. I am fairly certain that of

---

*   Matthews' autobiography , Headline, 2001

Jack Matthews
N.S.C. 1912

. . . A Dinne

to Honour Mr. Stanl

on the occasion of his S

in Professional

at the Club Headquarters

The Cafe Royal, W.1

Tuesday
18th September, 1956

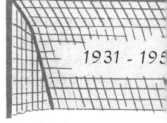

1931 - 195

tional *Sporting*

Club

Presentation

atthews

Jubilee

ıll

Stanley Matthews
N.S.C. 1956

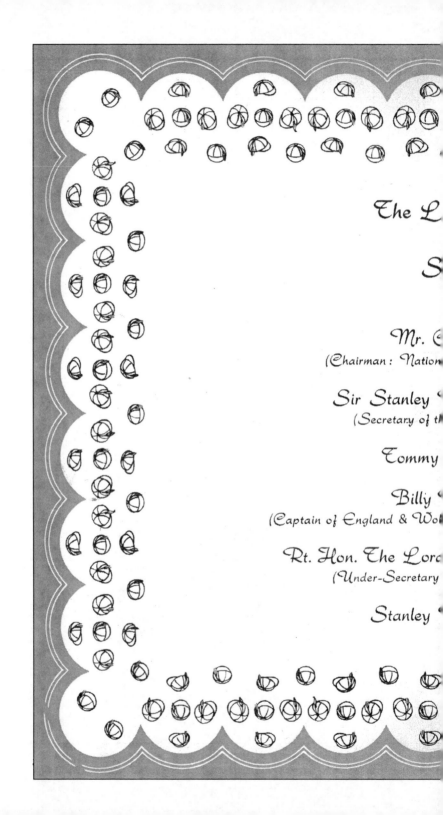

The L

S

Mr.
(Chairman: Nation

Sir Stanley
(Secretary of t

Tommy

Billy
(Captain of England & Wo

Rt. Hon. The Lord
(Under-Secretary

Stanley

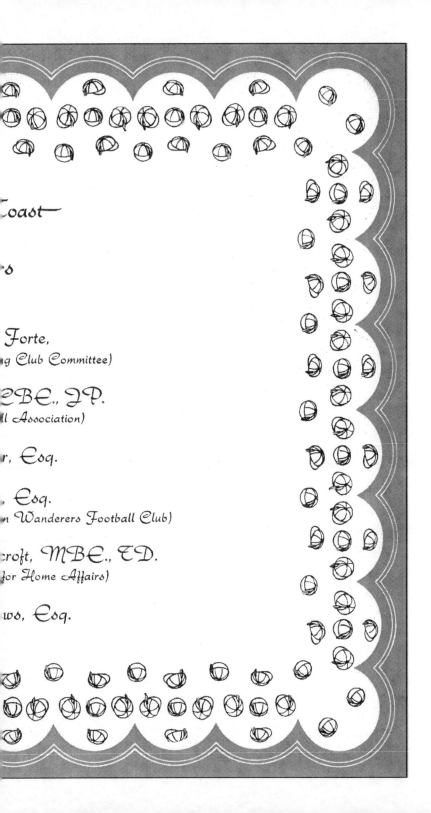

Coast

s

Forte,
g Club Committee)

MBE., JP.
l Association)

r, Esq.

, Esq.
n Wanderers Football Club)

croft, MBE., ED.
for Home Affairs)

ws, Esq.

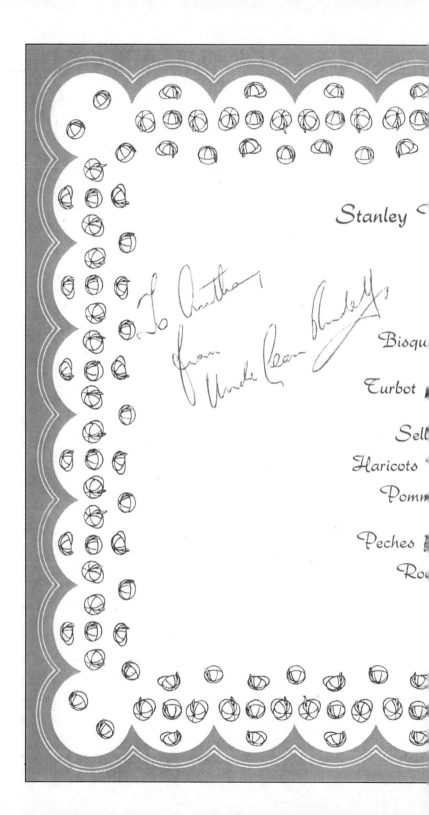

Stanley

To Anthony from Uncle ...

Bisqu

Turbot

Sell

Haricots

Pomm

Peches

Roc

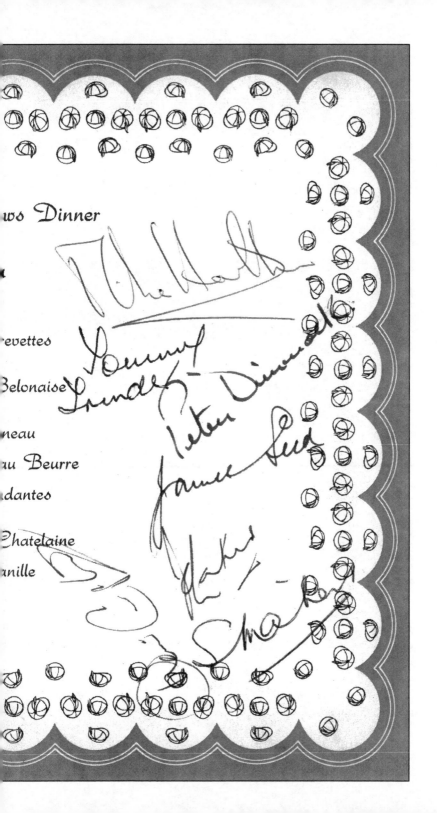

...ws Dinner

...revettes

...Belonaise

...neau

...u Beurre

...dantes

...Chatelaine

...anille

The Nation

The National Sporting Club is proud to
footballers of our time, to celebrate his Silve

It is nearly 27 years since Stanley bega
for Stoke City at the age of fifteen to work
Stoke Reserves, and made 22 appearances in
he signed as a professional, and soon after
at 19 and has since added another 76 caps
every footballer, gaining a Cup Winner's M

Throughout the world the name of Stan
"soccer" and only a few weeks ago a German
footballer outside of Germany. This has ha
and France—in fact, wherever soccer is play
Truly has he earned his title of "Ambassad
that such a distinguished company, not on
sports, have gathered here this evening to pa

It would seem that his brilliant footwo
many of the old members of the N.S.C. will
Garden, where he met and defeated some o
that the National Sporting Club should be

orting Club

night Stanley Matthews, one of the greatest
s a professional footballer.

headlines as the boy wonder when he signed
ce for a £1 a week. He turned out twice for
d XI at sixteen. On his seventeenth birthday
the first team. He was capped for England
ction. He has also achieved the ambition of
g for Blackpool.

ews has long been synonymous with the word
per Poll showed that he was the most popular
ore in Hungary, Yugoslavia, Holland, Belgium
ws has been named the player of the century.
h Sport" and it is a tribute to his popularity
wn contemporaries, but the leaders of other
o this remarkable personality.

erited from his father, Jack Matthews, whom
for his great fights at the old Club in Covent
boxers of his time, and so it is doubly fitting
o honour his famous son.

all the names on the programme – committee, speech makers and autographers — only Peter Dimmock is still alive at the time of writing. Dimmock, ninety last week (December 2010), was Head of BBC Outside Broadcasts (Coronation, Grand National etc) and a top sports presenter. The name of James Seed will only be known to sports fans of a certain age and you have to Google 'Jimmy Seed' to find details of the England soccer international and manager of various club sides. Jim Laker I have already mentioned earlier in the context of the Oval Test Match that year. This dinner was held three weeks after the test. Denis Compton and Stanley Matthews himself can easily be tracked down by interested readers, unless interested readers are defined as those who do not need to track the players down. Which leave Mike Hawthorn and Tommy Trinder. Driving a Ferrari, Hawthorn was the World Formula One champion in 1958 and, ironically enough, died in a road crash in 1959. Tommy 'you lucky people' Trinder everyone knew well from his radio appearances and his compèring the television show, Sunday Night at the London Palladium – Bruce Forsyth took over from him in 1958.

The Autographs (6)

Pete Murray and Jo Douglas hosted *Six-Five Special* (not 6-5 Special as I wrote in my album), perhaps the first television rock and roll programme for teenagers. It ran for most of 1957 and 1958, and one evening, probably in late 1958, armed with the hottest tickets in town, I went on the bus or by tube with Gill Posner, collecting her from her house in Rowdon Avenue, Willesden. I took her because she was pretty and sweet. She wasn't my 'girl friend'. I didn't have one and didn't know you were supposed to, not being precocious or even normal in that department. It would be more than three years before my body,

Pete Murray

let alone my mind, was in gear. (It must have been after Gill Posner that I embarked on a long-standing crush on Patricia Hammerson in neighbouring Brondesbury, another north-west London Jewish enclave). I made Gill, in her pink angora jumper, promise not to dance and such was the power of the ticket that she agreed but she broke her promise, dragging me in my beige pullover onto the dance floor to jive, and above all to be seen by friends and family, not to mention the viewing public. The star guest that evening was Laurie ('he's got the whole world in his hands') London, younger than me and much shorter. Perhaps that was why I didn't ask him for his autograph but instead got Pete Murray's. Later, London ran hotels.

On the same page as Pete Murray is Joyce Grenfell, an actress much admired for her monologues ('George, don't do that'). She recorded W. S. Gilbert and Hilaire Belloc verses with Stanley Holloway, another brilliant monologist. Heaven knows where I obtained her autograph – more thanks to Uncle Leon,

Joyce Grenfell

Jayne Mansfield

I suspect. On the next page we come to Jayne Mansfield, with a heart over the letter i instead of a dot. Again, I have no clue concerning its provenance, I never met her and in any case she wasn't my type, I preferred Jeanne Moreau and Juliette Greco: you get the picture. I did, however, meet the Platters at Golders Green Hippodrome, probably in 1958. It is strange that I recall obtaining their autographs but not the performance they gave there. I loved and loved their songs, which I am listening to on Spotify even as I type this section: 'Only You', 'The Great Pretender' (the 351st greatest song of all time, according to *Rolling Stone* and their only one in the list of 500), 'Twilight Time' and 'Smoke Gets in your Eyes'. By the time I met them, the group consisted of Tony Williams, David Lynch, Paul Robi, Herb Reed and Zola Taylor, of whom Lynch and Reed were the only survivors of the original line-up. Yet, however much I try to match the scrawls to the names, the only legible signature is Herb Reed's. I had to have all five signatures, for how many people even then could name them individually? This was a decade before the Beatles and the personalisation of fame and the quintet doubtless speeded up in order to meet the needs of all the teenagers waiting for them to sign the albums or in my case a piece of paper to be pasted in when I got home.

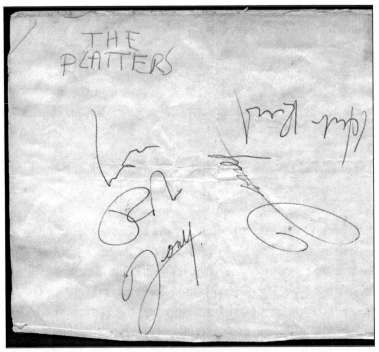

The Platters

Later the group would have trouble with their reputations after the men were busted for drugs and prostitution charges.

At the foot of the page after The Platters is the signature of Burt Lancaster, whose provenance will turn out to be the same as that of Jayne Mansfield. Above him is Reg Pearman, whom I remember meeting in Copenhagen near the statue of

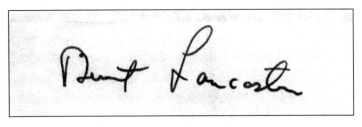

Burt Lancaster

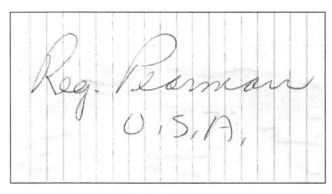

Reg Pearman

the Little Mermaid on a family holiday in the 1950s. I have a vague memory of finding his wallet on the ground. Perhaps I saw him drop it and ran over to give it to him, or how would I have known it was his? It must have emerged that he was an athlete – possibly in town for a race – and I have written 'athlete' on the piece of paper stuck into the album. Another vague memory is that he was a hurdler and so we google in anticipation: the only reference I can find to him is that in London in 1952 he was a member of the USA team which achieved the world record for the 4 x 400 meters relay. It lasted four years. Maybe he was also a 400 meter hurdler. He died on June 11th 2012, aged 89. He had, I hope, his memories, of the day he won the world record, although not, doubtless, of something that happened a year or two later at the Little Mermaid, when he made the day of a young autograph hunter who was surely not expecting to get lucky while on holiday with his parents and one or two sisters.

Six autographs to go. I remember attending a concert of Chris Barber's band and here is an autograph labelled 'Chris Barber's trumpeter', namely Pat Halcox. Cue to visit Spotify, where there is a short list under his own name and a long list under Barber. I click onto 'St Louis Blues' in the Halcox

Pat Halcox

list – from an album called 'Chris Barber at the Royal Festival Hall', maybe that was the concert I attended – and am transported by the Ottilie Patterson solo. Patterson, who died while I was correcting the proofs of this book, was a favourite of mine when I was young, along with Annie Ross of Lambert, Hendricks and Ross – I met Ross later at Arnold Wesker's house in Highgate at the farewell party of the poet Pablo Armando Fernandez – and Cleo Laine. Pat Halcox was a member of the band for half a century. He names as his early influence Mugsy Spanier on cornet. Like Barber, he is eighty this year. Other names associated with the band were Monty Sunshine on clarinet who died recently and Lonnie Donegan, whose songs are as redolent of my teen years as the Goon Show and this very autograph album. Playing Annie Ross's 'C'est Si Bon', I am wondering why her French accent is so atrocious. It has to be deliberate. I shall catch her on my next trip to Manhattan where, at eighty, she is still singing. Her version of the eponymous Rogers and Hart song is jazzier than Ella's – the touchstone – and includes the second and saucy chorus: 'we'll go to Greenwich / which modern men itch / to be free' . . . 'we'll bathe at Brighton / the fish I'll frighten

/ when I'm in / my bathing suit so thin / we'll make the shellfish grin / fin to fin'. Blossom Dearie (whom my friend James Hogan once saw in Hendon) sings it much more slowly than Ella and Annie, and uses the same words as Ella. Sandra Caron in her book on Alma understandably includes the poll of Outstanding British Feminine Singers conducted among *New Musical Express* readers in 1956. Alma came top with 9,466 votes followed immediately by Lita Roza and Anne Skelton. Ottilie Paterson was eighteenth with 457 votes, Annie Ross twenty third with 332 votes. I have heard (of) all twenty five singers, except the last, Annette Klooger, who can be found on Spotify and YouTube sounding a little like Alma Cogan.

The only politicians in the album sign in as 'E. Shinwell' and 'E. Burton'. The autographs of these Labour members of parliament came from my father, who moved in Labour Party circles, mainly on a local level, where he stood as a candidate for St Paul's Ward, Finchley in an election in, I think, 1955. There is a photo of him with a pipe, taken for the local press to use (aping Harold Wilson, always photographed with a pipe in public, whereas he smoked cigars in private). I have written about my own Labour Party experiences in *A/M* and in *Zigzag*. Manny Shinwell, born

Emanuel Shinwell

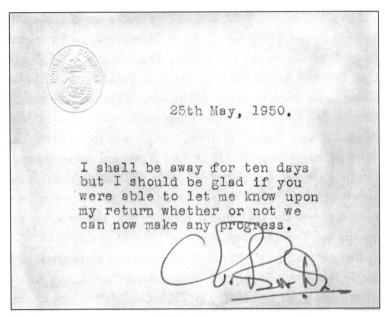

25th May, 1950.

I shall be away for ten days
but I should be glad if you
were able to let me know upon
my return whether or not we
can now make any progress.

Elaine Burton

in 1884 and who lived till he was more than a hundred, was Minister of Fuel and Power in Clement Attlee's first government and therefore responsible for the nationalisation of the mines. He later became Secretary of State for War and finally Minister of Defence in Attlee's short-lived second government in 1950. Shinwell's parents moved from Spitalfields to Glasgow when he was a child. He was a tough character, having been formed by his experiences as a trade union and political activist amidst the great poverty of Red Clydeside, a hard school. On one occasion he punched a Tory MP for telling him, a Jewish MP, to go back to Poland. Elaine Burton is now completely forgotten. Her signature is appended to a proper autograph message typed on a House of Commons card and dated 25th May 1950: 'I shall be away for ten days but I should be glad if you were able to let me know upon my return whether or not we can make any progress'. What was that about? Whatever, it was written three months after the 1950 general election which returned Labour to power with a reduced majority, and brought Elaine into the house as member for Coventry South, where she defeated a Tory who is remembered for having introduced a road safety measure when Minister of Transport, namely the beacons which were popularly known by part of his surname: Sir Leslie Hore-Belisha. In 1945, Burton was the defeated Common Wealth candidate in Hendon South, next door the constituency where I grew up, Finchley, although the former family house is once again in Hendon South after boundary changes. (I am reminded of the Sunday painter who, following similar changes, complained that she could not start painting Oxfordshire landscapes after a lifetime of painting Berkshire landscapes).

Hore-Belisha became Secretary of State for War in 1937 – even though his being Jewish meant that Chamberlain thought there was a risk he would be too zealous in anti-German attitudes – finally introduced conscription in 1939 after long prevarication by Chamberlain. His reforms of the armed forces infuriated the military establishment 'and this sentiment was passed down to the lower ranks. In the early months of World War II, he banned or attempted to ban a popular yet anti-semitic song which had been widely sung by the armed forces, to the tune of 'Onward Christian Soldiers':

> Onward Christian Soldiers,
> You have nought to fear.
> Israel Hore-Belisha
> Will lead you from the rear.
> Clothed by Monty Burton,
> Fed on Lyons pies;
> Die for Jewish freedom
> As a Briton always dies.

Earlier I raised the issue of the provenance of my autographs of Eddie Cantor, Burt Lancaster and Jayne Mansfield. I have solved the problem with a glance at the next signature: Fernandel. The signature is on a card invitation to the world premiere of *Paris Holiday* at the London Pavilion on Thursday, February 27th 1958 at 8.30pm, starring Bob Hope, Anita Ekberg, Martha Hyer and the French actor himself. Written by hand on the card is G2, the seat number, a good seat, of the person who obtained the autograph. The clue to the provenance is the logo 'United Artists'. Our family friend, Joe Pole, as I have already said, was Public Relations Officer for United Artists and would have given the card to me or given it to my parents to give to me. A swift visit to Google reveals that Cantor, Lancaster and Mansfield all made films produced by United Artists. Q. E. D.

We must have made a family visit to Woburn Abbey because

Fernandel

I have a postcard of the Abbey signed 'Bedford' by its owner, the thirteenth Duke. I do have a vivid memory of visiting Hatfield House and climbing a tree. I can still see the tree in my mind's eye, and only a visit to both great houses will resolve the issue as to whether the visit was in fact to Woburn Abbey.

The Duke of Bedford

Not a priority. Which brings me to the final signature in the album: 'Neville Shute Norway', who is better known by the first two names as a writer of popular novels, many of which I read in my teens, borrowed either from East Finchley public library or the mobile library off South Square in the Suburb near my house. Years later, the most helpful public librarian in the world (i.e. in North London), Stephanie Lafferty, would work there. I met Neville Shute at the Middleway house of my friend Peter Goodeve, whose father Sir Charles Goodeve was a friend of Shute's. There the novelist signed my copy of *No Highway* and also signed his name directly into the album, one of only three not stuck in or otherwise inserted, along with Alex Ehrlich and Zoltan Berczik. It now seems to me extraordinary that I did not carry the album around with me.

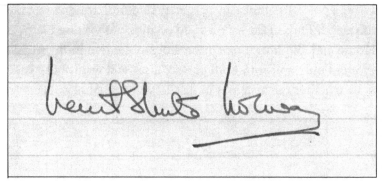

Neville Shute Norway

I am fairly sure that Shute signed in 1959. He is, along with the loosely inserted Eddie Cantor, the final person to feature in my album. It seems appropriate that I met him in person and that he signed on the page itself. Quite by accident, therefore, I signed off as a collector with a writer, at an age when I had no idea I would become one myself.

Twenty or twenty five years later I would encourage my son Nathaniel to collect autographs and, like Joe Pole and my uncle Leon before me (and for me), I used my contacts to help him get famous names, such as the then Prime Minister of New Zealand, David Lange, to whom I had written on the issue of nuclear weapons, something which was preoccupying me in the early eighties as much as it did when I went on the final stage of the first Aldermaston march in 1958. I wonder if I mentioned Aldermaston to Neville Shute whose pioneering post-nuclear-war novel *On the Beach* was published in 1957 and made into a film in 1959. I do wonder about the surname, Norway. Shute's father Arthur Hamilton Norway was born in Cornwall and was the Deputy Head of the Post Packet Service in Dublin at the time of the Black and Tan Rebellion. He was an author himself. Google: 'Recorded in the spellings of Northway and Norwar, this is an English surname of great antiquity. Famous for being associated with the late author, Neville Shute Norway, it has nothing directly to do with Norsemen or Vikings, or indeed the modern inhabitants of the country Norway. The name is of Olde English pre 7th century; it is of residential origins and in most cases describes a person who lived "north of the road".' As I said, I met Neville in Middleway (See *The Arithmetic of Memory* for many memories of the street where I grew up). I wonder if he realised that the street was between Northway and Southway.

Conclusion

If I were writing a full-scale book on autographs I would perhaps include a section on the autographs owned by friends of mine, for example John Seed, who kept score for Durham when he was young. In those days Durham was a 'minor county'. The league also contained some second elevens of major county teams. Seed has the autographs of many cricketers and also footballers but there is no overlap with my collection. It turns out, however, that he is the great-nephew of Jimmy Seed, who is the least well-known of the signatures on my *pièce de résistance*. Then there is Paul Buck who, like me, owns Johnny Leach but says Denis Compton has gone missing from his bunch. I would once have envied him Diane Rowe and Harry Secombe. I could have done a piece of cod research and asked a large number of friends about their autograph experience when young but I cannot resist telling something that happened on a recent visit to Paris while I was in Yves Bonnefoy's flat, waiting for his daughter Mathilde Olivia and her husband Dirk to turn up so that we could go out for dinner. I mentioned my album to Bonnefoy. He left the room and returned shortly with a book and something else. The latter was the signature of Stéphane Mallarmé given to Bonnefoy by a collector and which Yves had framed. What is remarkable about it is that the poet has greatly elongated the final e in a playful and yet purposeful way. The book which Bonnefoy showed me was an anthology, *The Second Book of the Rhymers Club* (1894), given to him by the daughter of Jean Wahl, Bonnefoy's philosophy teacher at the Sorbonne in the immediate post-war years. It has the following inscription:

> For Miss Maud Gonne
> from her friend
> W. B. Yeats

That is a major-league example of what book dealers call an association copy and the fact that it is now owned by a great French poet who is himself a translator of Yeats adds to the interest. Rick Gekoski, a specialist in association copies, tells me that the first *Book of the Rhymers Club* (1892), with the identical dedication, fetched a very large sum of money at Sothebys New York in 2004. The group met upstairs at the Cheshire Cheese in Fleet Street between 1891 and 1894 (the same room where Michael Schmidt of Carcanet sometimes arranges book launches); Yeats – who found the Club meetings 'always decorous and often dull' – Dowson and Arthur Symons were among the founders. Oscar Wilde occasionally attended, but only in private houses. The group staggered on until 1904. When, out of curiosity, I told Bonhams about Yves Bonnefoy's copy, the charming and intelligent woman in the books department practically had an orgasm. I could not help thinking of Maud Gonne, but restrained myself. The copy is not for sale, sadly for the Bonhams woman. Some years ago, Gekoski sold Eliot's *Poems 1920* signed to Virginia Woolf and a copy of *The Waste Land* signed to Wyndham Lewis. It is a statement of the bleeding obvious that such associations are not possible on iPad, but I still want to make the statement. Even so, books will survive into the electronic age without my advocacy. I know only two people who prefer reading books on the screen, but sadly their tribe, like Abou ben Adhem's, will increase, although unlike him their names will not be written in the book of gold.

I am well pleased I found my autograph album, an endotic anthropological document from my teen years half a century ago. In those days my present age of sixty eight would have been considered old but in 2010, well, when I visited my uncle Jack Simon recently – he is ninety nine – the name of my grandmother Rebecca Rosenberg, his mother in law, came up. I mentioned that she seemed old to me when she was hardly older than I am now. 'You're old too', said Jack. This startled me into silence before I said, 'no, you're old'. 'Tony, you're old, I'm very old'.

Why do young people collect signatures of famous people? Perhaps they do it less these days, given that it is so easy to photograph with a mobile phone. But in those days it was a way of capturing a trace of the hero or heroine whose presence cast a spell (as in the first meaning of the word glamour) and, what's more, involved personal contact, however fleeting. On the other hand, you still see, for example, players signing albums and programmes at Wimbledon as they leave the court.

At the time I was not (thank goodness) to know that one day the album would generate nostalgia, the compost of texts such as this, but I enjoyed the fleeting contact with thirty two signers out of my sixty. Nor was I to know that one day I would own a publisher's archive with letters, handwritten and typed, from authors, some famous, of around one hundred and sixty books, though these do not mean more to me than the forgotten cricketers of my youth.

The computer I am writing on contains emails from many of these authors. In the interregnum between posted letters and emails there were the faxes. I have seen in a New York storage space rented by my friend Mike Heller a large pile of yellowing faxes, matching his faxes which I have here. And the hundreds of phonecalls? Three alone survive on a small cassette which I kept: the words of a very angry lover, all spoken on one dire evening (('quoth she, and whistles thrice'). I took the cassette round to my friend Musa and we played them many times, with me hoping against hope that the third message was less angry than the first. To no avail. I was clutching at straws. This kind of behaviour was brilliantly anatomised in Barthes' *A Lover's Discourse*, but such craziness is a signature from another book, another music, another life, another world.

And the humble autograph album? It portrays the world of a London teenager from the 1950s. I asked in my introduction if my grandchildren would one day keep autograph albums. I doubt it but, all the same, I hope I live long enough and in good enough health to enjoy the teen years of Charlie and Leah, who are among the dedicatees of this book. The future is even more difficult to imagine than the past. As for the present, which partakes of both, it is, for that reason, still more opaque. Which is one reason why I have attempted to read this rare surviving document from my childhood. You have to get out of the compound sometimes, as Ron Mueck likes to say. He, however, is referring to physical displacement, I'm talking about time: there's a lot to be said for the present, but it raises issues that belong elsewhere.

Postscript: one of my Stamp Albums

Here is the only surviving stamp album from my days as a collector. It is one of those hard-covered spring-back binders which later on I and everyone I knew would use for storing poems or drafts of poems. This binder, however, is a specialist one, the Senator from Stanley Gibbons, still in the same location in the Strand as when I was a customer. Appropriately enough, Gibbons himself was born in 1840, the year of the first two adhesive postage stamps, the penny black and twopenny blue. A swift google reveals that the Senator binder is still on the market: 'Standard sized Spring-Back unpadded binder which is decoratively gold blocked on the spine with album name. Album contains 75 white cartridge acid free leaves with feint quadrilled field. Leaf size 251 x 282mm (9.88" x 11.13"). Optional glassine interleaving is also available.' Mine has the interleaving. All the stamps have been carefully attached to the page by what I recall were called stamp hinges. This is my British Empire album. Under Hong Kong, I find a surprise. I could have sworn on oath that I finished stamp collecting around the time I finished with autographs and cigarette cards, that is at the end of the fifties before my gap year and university. Yet here is a stamp commemorating the Red Cross centenary: 1863–1963. I am certain I was not actively collecting stamps in 1963. Maybe I added a stamp or two in later years. And where did the stamps come from? Did I buy them from Stanley Gibbons or was I given them, or a mixture of the two? I didn't know anyone in the territories who would have written to me and in any case many of the stamps antedate my lifetime. However, under Jamaica, we find not only stamps but a stamped air-letter envelope addressed to J. J. Nunes Vaz Esq., / H.C. Rudolf & Company / Balfour House / Finsbury Pavement / London EC2 / England. The late John Jacob Nunes Vaz, known as Jack Nunes, was my father's first partner and for some years only partner, and became senior partner on my father's death in 1986. (He called me in and said: 'the party's over, Anthony, no more free accounts'. That was a shock to my system and my bank account). His surname, like that of my friend the poet Robert Vas Dias, is a classic Portuguese name. Both are Sephardi Jews whose ancestors hailed from Portugal (the Anglo-Jewish equivalent of coming over on the Mayflower). Quite likely a lot of the stamps were given to me by my father. I recall now that he said it was interesting to collect not only stamps but also the envelope they arrived on. I now reckon this was good advice, but sadly there is only the one in this surviving album.

The album begins with Aden. All headings have been pasted in from some set of names, doubtless supplied by Stanley Gibbons. But the Aden stamps have been removed. Someone, and it is not in my handwriting, has written descriptions of the missing stamps, for example: 'Aidrus Mosque, Crater North, worth 10d [i.e. ten old pennies], King George VI 1939'. There are three pages for Australia. The stamps on the first page have been removed, leaving only the hinges. Pages two and three contain a miscellany of stamps, showing people or places or native animals or commemorating events such as the 1935 twentieth anniversary of Anzac, the Australia and New Zealand Army Corps of the First World War. On page three, the same hand as on the Aden page has written descriptions of the stamps which are still there, including one which commemorates the Golden Jubilee of Guiding in 1960. A phone call to my sister Annie elicits the information that it was not her. One of the Australia stamps has Elizabeth and Philip which I don't recall seeing on a UK stamp. But I'm no expert, having done nothing more active than appear on a stamp, as mentioned earlier. Next come the Bahamas, Barbados, Basutoland, Bechuanaland, British Honduras, British Solomon Islands, Zanzibar [back to front and obviously reinserted in the wrong place], British Somaliland [empty], Brunei [whose Sultan I met years later in the lift of the Avenue Clinic where I was visiting the then Matron, my friend Diana May], Burma, Canada [three pages including all monarchs back to Edward VII, Ceylon, Cyprus, Dominica [a single $^1/_4$d or farthing stamp], Falkland Dependencies [including a stamp showing the John Biscoe, a ship used in the British Antarctic Survey], Fiji, Ghana, Gold Coast [pre-Ghana territory], Gibraltar.

There follow five pages of Great Britain: among them are stamps of Edward the eighth, 1948 Olympic commemoration stamps, 1851–1951 stamps for the Festival of Britain, and a

Churchill stamp, presumably issued in 1965 on his death – thus even later than the Hong Kong stamp in terms of my collecting span. Great Britain is followed by Hong Kong, Jamaica, Kenya/ Uganda/Tanganyika, which shared stamps, Kuwait and Leeward Islands. Malaya, Singapore, Johore, Straits Settlements and Penang are a group. Some of these have sultans on them, presumably after independence. Malta follows, one of the stamps over-printed with the words 'self-government 1947', then Mauritius, Montserrat, Muscat and a stamp of the Morocco Agencies marking the coronation of 1937 and overprinted with '15 centimes'. Apparently, Britain operated the post offices and bagged the stamps over to Gibraltar. Why was Great Britain running the post offices when Morocco was divided into a French and Spanish protectorate?★ We arrive at Newfoundland. I always thought the latter was part of Canada but it was a self-governing dominion from 1907 till 1934 when, broke, it voluntarily surrendered self-government and was governed and administered from London

★ Morocco Agencies (British Post Offices) (*Stanley Gibbons note supplied by John Brown courtesy of Antony Gray and abridged by me*) With the growth of trade and commerce during the 19th century European powers opened Post Offices or Postal Agencies in various ports along the Moroccan coast from the early 1850's onwards. French and, Spanish influence eventually became predominant leading to the protectorates of 1912. Before 1892 there was no indigenous postal service and those towns where there was no foreign agency were served by a number of private local posts which continued to flourish until 1900. The British, who had inaugurated a regular postal service between Gibraltar and Tangier or Tetuan in 1778, established their first postal agency in Tangier in 1857 within the precinct of the Legation. From 1858 all letters for Great Britain sent via the British Mail Packets from Gibraltar required franking with Great Britain stamps. In 1872 the Tangier office was relocated away from the Legation and the interpreter was appointed British Postal Agent. At the same time the agency was placed under the control of the Gibraltar postmaster. When the colonial posts became independent of the British GPO on 1 Jan 1886 Gibraltar retained responsibility for the Morocco Agencies.

until it became Canada's tenth province in 1949. An interesting feature of the four Newfoundland stamps I have is that along with a coronation stamp of 1937 featuring George VI and Elizabeth, two of them portray solo wives of a King (Mary and Elizabeth) and a third has the future Queen Elizabeth as a child. All of them were issued during the London phase of government. Perhaps the postal authorities had a brief window of freedom. The New South Wales page contains some of the oldest stamps in my album and feature Queen Victoria at a time when the state was a separate colony. I look at New Zealand with fresh eyes because my grandson Charlie and parents live there. God's Own is followed by Nigeria, North Borneo, Northern Rhodesia and Nyasaland Protectorate and Rhodesia/Nyasaland. Perhaps the most beautiful stamps in the book are from St Helena, one of Britain's few remaining official colonies. The book ends with Saint Lucia, Sarawak, Seychelles, Sierra Leone, South Africa / Suid Africa, South Australia, Southern Rhodesia, Tanganyika, Tonga, Trinidad / Tobago. Farewell, stamp album, I am glad to have renewed acquaintance after many years. You weren't even lost.

Lightning Source UK Ltd.
Milton Keynes UK
UKOW032143200613

212548UK00001BA/4/P